Library of Congress Cataloging-in-Publication Data

Nolan, Bernard T., Deadly Skies: The Air War in Europe 1940-1945,

Summary: A history of the European air war in WWII with detailed descriptions of the aircraft and battles by a bomber pilot who was there.

ISBN: 1939282217
Published by Miniver Press, LLC, McLean Virginia

First edition August 2013

DEADLY SKIES

THE AIR WAR IN EUROPE 1940-1945

[signature: Bernard Nolan]

By

BERNARD T. NOLAN
LTCOL USAF, RETIRED

Illustrations by Matthew Holness
One generation passeth away, and
Another generation cometh: but the
Earth abideth for ever.
Ecclesiastes 1:4

Dedication:

Honoring those airmen who gave their lives for our freedom

ACKNOWLEDGEMENT

Deadly Skies descends from a lecture I present to various groups with a bent for aviation history. Colin Smith of Vector Fine Art Prints in England suggested that I put it in book form. My lecture focuses on the USAAF Eighth Air Force in the Second World War. Aiming for a wider market in the UK, *Deadly Skies* has been broadened to connect the Eighth Air Force, the RAF and the Luftwaffe in the breadth of the entire war in Western Europe, focusing on its cost in terms of death and destruction.

In writing *Deadly Skies*, I am indebted to several authors as research sources that provided me a guiding path for the undertaking. This book could not have been written without them. They are my prime sources for *Deadly Skies:*

Lancaster, The Biography	Tony Iveson
With Wings Like Eagles	Michel Korda
Fire and Fury	Randall Hansen
Masters of the Air	Donald L. Miller
The Mighty Eighth	Roger A. Freeman
The Final Hours	Johannes Steinhoff

In Appendix 1, I list the above books and others that have served as research sources for this work.

I also acknowledge the work of budding aviation artist Matthew Holness, whose ideas and original illustrations adorn each chapter heading and elsewhere in the book. Kudos also go to my daughter and editor Pamela Nolan, to Sunny, my wife of 67 years, and son Tom Nolan, who are my prime critics assisting with context for my textual output. Thanks go also to Frank Ceresi who found a publishing path for *Deadly Skies*, and Nell Minow for undertaking that task.

Author's note: Some of the material in this book has been previously published in *Isaiah's Eagles Rising, A Generation of Airmen*, Xlibris, second edition 2012.

TABLE OF CONTENTS

DEADLY SKIES

BY BERNARD NOLAN

PROLOGUE

May 28, 1944

We were now headlong into the black hell. I watched a stricken B-24 in its death throes pass below me. My thoughts turned to the past – a kid from the great depression, driven like so many of my generation by a burning obsession to fly. I was not ready for what I saw as we turned from the initial point to the heading that would take us to the target and ten more minutes in hell. The sky was alive with black pulsating images with red-orange cores. The intercom was deadly quiet, each of us ten souls aboard alone in our fear. Mesmerized with the exploding black clouds called flak over a place called Lutzkendorf in Germany, I now experienced a Faust moment; to realize my obsession, I had traded my soul to the Devil.

Some 35 years later, my wife Sunny and I were invited to a reception at the National Air and Space Museum by Colonel Don Lopez, who at the time was a member of the museum's staff. The reception featured the original paintings by the noted British aviation artist Robert Taylor.

I was no stranger to Taylor's talent. In fact, I have prints of two of his paintings: one called "Mission Completed" portraying an Eighth Air Force B-17 about to land, hangs proudly in our family gathering room, along with two others by the American master Keith Ferris. "Mission Completed" bears the signatures of six USAAF Medal of Honor recipients. The second Taylor print, "A Gathering of Eagles," bearing signatures of notable World War II airmen including Peter Townsend, hangs in my daughter Pamela's living room.

Peter Townsend was present at the Air Museum reception, as were many other prominent veterans of WW II. Townsend was a British fighter pilot in the Battle of Britain who gained notoriety as a suitor to Princess Margaret. I was deeply honored for the opportunity to talk to a pilot who actually flew and survived the Battle of Britain. When introduced to Townsend he expressed interest in my background with the Eighth in which he eschewed the very idea of flying bombers.

What then followed was a meeting that I will never forget. Don Lopez was well aware of the fact that I had flown both the B-24 and the B-17 in combat. Don approached me during the reception and said, "Barney, Adolf Galland is here tonight. I was telling him about your experience with both the B-24 and B-17. He said he would like to talk to you." Galland's curiosity was obviously aroused at my flying both these bombers in combat during the war. "Adolf Galland, *wow*," I thought, leader of the Luftwaffe fighter command in WW II. It would be like meeting the likes of Lindberg or Doolittle. I had no idea Galland was present. My initial reaction was visions of the feared Abbeville Kids and their Bf 109s. Now *my* curiosity was aroused, and upon coming face-to-face with Galland, I intended to go into my pitch mode, comparing the two aircraft that I assumed to be Galland's interest. When we did meet, Don made the introduction and disappeared. Galland and I shook hands and I recall a moment of hesitation as we regarded one another. He was gracious, easy to talk to and I sensed that I liked him, at the same time thinking about how much we shared. With regard to the conversion from the B-24 to the B-17, Galland did not ask the question I expected. Not Galland. He asked "Why?"

For context, Eighth Bomber Command had three divisions. The first division was equipped with B-17s, the second division B-24s and the third a mix of 14 B-24 and B-17 bomb groups. Galland of course knew this, but his question was why did Generals Curtis LeMay and Jimmy Doolittle replace the third division B-24 groups with the B-17. I felt blind-sided – I had no clue as to why, other than to suggest that the B-17 performed better in the combat environment of Western Europe. Galland seemed satisfied with that response, and we parted company. I have since made it a point to seek the deeper reasoning that went into the decision. LeMay wanted to standardize both operational procedures and logistic support for a single aircraft type. Simply put, he picked the B-17 over the B-24 because it was a better performer. We will examine the comparison between the two in operational performance later in this book.

In retrospect, the encounters with three pilots that night at the National Air and Space Museum – a German, a Brit and an American – suggests three paths I will follow in this work: to discuss how the WW II air campaign in Western Europe unfolded, how it ended, and its cost in terms of human life – not only for the aircrews in those unfriendly skies, but the innumerable innocents who suffered through the carnage in European cities caused by bombing. In so doing, my focus will be on the Royal Air Force, the U.S. Army Eighth Air Force and the Luftwaffe

.

Hurricanes to the Intercept

CHAPTER 1:   THINGS TO COME

The Bomber Will Always Get Through

It is said that World War II was an extension of World War I. True enough, in that the Versailles Treaty humiliated Germany and paved the way for the rise of Hitler. There is no intent in this book to wander into the morass of European politics and mind-sets of the time, but insofar as the WW II air campaign in Western Europe is concerned, it is necessary to examine aviation development and the thrust of thinking that set the stage for what ensued.

The seeds that gave birth to the WW II air campaign in Western Europe were planted long before 1930. The idea of destroying a nation's capacity and will to make war emerged with Union General William Sherman's 1864 march through Georgia in the American Civil War. Sherman cut through the underbelly of the Confederacy and laid waste to everything in his path, forerunner of what in WW II was later called a "scorched earth policy." With the advent of the airplane, the idea of total warfare began to take root in a different format. WW I brought the first practical application of air power in the strategic sense with Germany's rigid airship attacks on Great Britain. They began with Zeppelin attacks on England in January 1915 with terrorism as the objective – burn London to the ground. The phrase echoes Giulio Douhet (1869-1930), Italian general and air power theorist who professed a dramatic build up of aircraft capable of bombing cities when Italy entered the war in 1915. By late summer 1915, after eight months of German attacks and significant British losses, nothing of military advantage was accomplished. The panic expected of the British populace did not surface, but the campaign with the German rigid air ships went on to the war's conclusion with negligible military or political results. In all, 140 rigids were used on offensive operations. Two thirds of these were destroyed in action, storms and accidents. No wonder, considering the vulnerability of a huge engine driven gas bag with millions of cubic feet of highly flammable gas subjected to incendiary bullets — all it took was a spark. Even the process of navigating at high altitudes in heavy winds that drew them off course underscores the flawed character of the concept. However, during WW I, 220 tons of bombs were dumped on England by Zeppelins causing 557 deaths and 1,538 injuries, plus 30 million dollars in property damage.

Despite all that, the air raids would continue with the Gotha and Zeppelin Giant aircraft when the rigids failed. All told, there were 52 attacks with these aircraft on Great Britain showering 2,772 bombs randomly on targets, amounting to 73 tons of explosives. These air attacks on London never even came close to achieving any positive results and did little in the way of endorsing this strategy, yet they were still disruptive to life in London, and 857 would perish with injuries three times that number. Even so, the people of London were not cowed, nor would they be during the Blitz in WW II.

A common mindset was forming in England, however, perhaps begun by former Prime Minister Stanley Baldwin's speech to Parliament on 10 November 1932. Dominating the Conservative political front between the two World Wars, his speech capsulized the attitude that there was no real defense against aircraft bombing cities during war, hence, *the bomber will always get through*.

The Prophets

Somehow, with so little benefit shown, the strategic possibilities of air power began to grow. Air strategy theorists like Italy's Giulio Douhet, England's Hugh "Boom" Trenchard, Marshal of the Royal Air Force in 1927, and our own Billy Mitchell, U.S. Army

General and father of the U.S. Air Force, emerged in the 1920s to expound on the potential of the aircraft as the ultimate strategic weapon. The aircraft was now being envisioned as the instrument of warfare that would deny a nation's capability to make war by destroying its industrial infrastructure and cowing its population with psychological disruption.

In the 1930s, the specter of mass destruction from the skies was savagely displayed with Japan's indiscriminate use of air power against China and the German air attacks in Spain during that country's civil war. The aerial attack on the Spanish city of Guernica was Hitler's lesson in how to destroy a city – the proving ground, if you like, for Hitler's new *Luftwaffe*. In the U.S., the application of strategic air power became doctrine even though the means of its delivery were still on the drawing boards. The destruction and suffering resulting from these episodes fed the literary and propaganda mills worldwide, conjuring up the image of helpless cities laid to waste. H.G. Wells' science fiction book, adapted into a film, *The Shape of Things to Come*, portrays a common frame of mind that consumed the Western world in that era.

Twenty-five years would pass after WW I before the advance of technology would even permit the test of the strategic air power theory. Even when massed strategic air power was applied from 1943 to 1945, this alone would not win the war in Europe, nor would the bomber always get through. For all the horrific destruction rained on Germany by the RAF and Eighth Air Force, German war production never ceased. Nor did its people panic any more in the fire storms that claimed so many of their cities than in those of London during the Blitz, the extension of the Nazi *blitzkrieg* that engulfed Poland and France in 1939 and 1940. It took the atomic bomb to bring the theory to reality.

Supermarine S.6 Racer—Early Prototype for the Spitfire

CHAPTER 2   THE INTERIM

The Locust Years – that is what Winston Churchill called them – were the years between the two world wars. The fearful idea that the bomber would always get through became a source of consummate dread for British politicians, at the same time influencing planning considerations in the RAF Air Council, as well as the thinking of Marshal Trenchard. Prime Minister Stanley Baldwin held the same thoughts – "the only defense is offense." Yet throughout the 1920s and early 1930s, Fighter Command was the pet of the Air Council, the governing body of the RAF. In the U.K., the two ideas, bombers versus fighters, were at odds with the drive to develop and plan an air strategy.

The Schneider Trophy

The advance of aviation technology has always been driven by the shopworn phrase "higher, faster and farther," a notion that would ingrain itself in the international political and military scene as WW II approached. WW I barnstorming and innovations such as mail delivery and passenger service led to new applications in aviation, but in terms of the explosion of its technology on the eve of WW II, speed was the major force, and the Schneider Trophy became its stage. The Schneider Trophy races date back to 1911 when one Jaques Schneider, a French financier, balloonist and aviation enthusiast announced a racing competition with a prize of $1,000.00 dollars as the draw. Competition was to focus on seaplanes, and France, Italy, the UK and the U.S. were the competitors. In 1914 Britain won with a Sopwith Tabloid clocking 86.7 mph. In 1920 Italy won with a flying boat at 107.1 mph. Italy won again in 1921 with a Macchi at 117.8 mph. The British entry in 1922, the Supermarine Company's Sea Lion II won at 145.63. The U.S. entered the competition in 1923 and won in a Curtis CR-3 at

177.27. The Curtis engine was a factor in the upgrading speed. In 1925, Jimmy Doolittle averaged 232.57, but an Italian Macchi won with a speed of 246.5. In 1927 Britain won again, clocking 281.66. In 1929 Reginald Mitchell – designer of the Spitfire – won the prize by replacing the Supermarine S.6 in the Napier Lion with a new engine developed by Rolls Royce. This engine would lead to the renowned Merlin. Indeed, the pontooned Supermarine S.6 was an early prototype for the Spitfire. By the late 1920s aircraft designs were now featuring sleek aluminum skinned monoplanes with continuing advances in engine performance. Biplanes were a thing of the past, and military applications would find their way into such technological advances.

The Innovators

Among the aeronautical innovators pertinent to this discussion were British pioneers Reginald Mitchell for the Supermarine Spitfire and Sydney Camm for the Hawker Hurricane, and two Avro Company men, Roy Dobson (managing director) and Roy Chadwick (chief designer) for the Avro Manchester and its offspring, the Lancaster, one of the most successful bombers of WW II. The Manchester had basic aerodynamic design features similar to its offspring but was a bit smaller. It was powered by two Rolls Royce Vulture engines – essentially four in line engines driving a common crankshaft. Much was expected of the Vulture, but the engine performed poorly, as did the early flights of the Manchester. Rolls-Royce had given up on the Vulture with the end of production in the offing and thus the end of the Manchester. Chadwick contended that he could produce a four engine bomber based on the Manchester to be designated the Manchester III. The four engines would be Merlins. Design work proceeded accordingly, and changes involved increased spans of the wing and tail plane – now called Type 683. Within the Air Ministry the Handley Page Halifax had the edge. Had Avro production on the

Manchester ended, their production lines would be changed to produce the Halifax. However, Dobson and Chadwick made their case with the Air Ministry and found support for a go ahead which would emerge as the Lancaster. Aside from the B-29 that came later, this aircraft would emerge in the European theatre as the premier bomber of WW II, with far more capability in speed and payload than its contemporaries.

Reginald Mitchell's Supermarine S.6 single-engine, single-seat racing seaplane was an early prototype for the Spitfire. In 1931 the S.6 had set world speed records for both seaplanes and land planes. Mitchell's designs drew the interest of the RAF. His 1931 Trophy plane featured the most advanced Rolls-Royce engine of the time, which would evolve as the Merlin. Mitchell and the Supermarine Company were drawn to the Air Ministry's design specification which called for proposals for a new single engine day and night fighter. Mitchell went through several design modifications before the lines of the Spitfire began to appear as a single wing aircraft with an enclosed cockpit and retractable landing gear. Bear in mind that much of this effort was promoted by Air Marshal Hugh Dowding, commander of RAF Fighter Command during the Battle of Britain, and flew in the face of conventional Air Staff thinking regarding the development of bombers.

The prototype Spitfire made its first flight on 15 March 1936. Dowding inspected the aircraft with the conclusion that Mitchell had produced a winged jewel. Rolls-Royce at this point had developed the PV XII that would be married to the Spitfire airframe and become the Merlin "bird of prey," with modifications made by Mitchell to accommodate the added weight. The Spitfire as we now know it had arrived.

As the Spitfire was in the development phase, Hawker Aircraft's Sydney Camm was designing the Hurricane in response to the Air Ministry's order for a prototype. Camm's design of a thick wing responded to the incorporation of eight 30-caliber machine guns. The landing gear would fold outward from the fuselage to facilitate easier handling characteristics. Camm's design would also feature the Merlin engine. The Hurricane flew for the first time a year before the Spitfire. By 1937, Hurricane's were on the scene in RAF squadrons. Hugh Dowding made his own inputs for modifications, calling for bullet proof glass to protect the pilots and ducted heating to the wings to keep machine guns from seizing at high altitude.

It is interesting to note that the Hawker Hurricane, overshadowed by the Spitfire, "became renowned during the Battle of Britain, accounting for 60 percent of the RAF's air victories in the battle, and served in all the major theatres of the Second World War."

The Messerschmitt Bf 109

Wilhelm Emil "Willy" Messerschmitt stands even today as one of the lions of aircraft design and development – with his innovative mind, I liken him to Kelly Johnson of our Lockheed company. Born in Frankfurt am Main in1898, Willy is best known for the development of the Luftwaffe's Bf 109, Germany's renowned air-to-air fighter of WW II, although not necessarily its best performer. The Focke-Wulf 190, to come later, had an edge in performance. Designed by Messerschmitt and Robert Lusser, the Bf 109 is more commonly called the Me 109. The designation Bf refers to the Bayerische Flugzeugwerke (Bavarian Aircraft Factory – BFW) where it was initially produced. In 1938 the Bf designation was changed to Me in honor of Messerschmitt when he took control of the company. Thus later designs, e.g., 210, 410, 163, 262, all took the Me prefix. The Bf 109, along with the Spitfire and Hurricane, was among the emerging all metal, low wing, retractable landing gear and closed canopy fighter aircraft designs appearing in the mid-1930s that would revolutionize aerial combat. The 109 was the first of these revolutionary fighters to experience combat operations when it was deployed by the Luftwaffe to Spain during the Spanish Civil War. The Luftwaffe gained significant tactical experience in Spain.

The prototype Bf 109 made its maiden flight with a Rolls-Royce Kestrel engine in May of 1935. The Kestrel engine substituted for the Junkers Jumo since the latter was delayed in production. Acceptance flights were completed at Rechlin, the airfield bordering Germany's research and development center at Peenemunde. The Bf 109 was selected by the Luftwaffe after competition with the Focke-Wulf (Fw) 159, Heinkel (He) 112 and the Arado (Ar) 80. In March 1936 the *Reichsluftahrtministerium* (Reich Aviation Ministry – RLM) learned that the British Spitfire had been ordered into production and quickly gave the order to begin production on the Bf 109.

Over the course of WW II, more than 10,000 of these aircraft were produced, appearing in variants A through K. The Bf 109 E "Emil" was the workhorse during the Battle of Britain. This version was equipped with a Daimler-Benz E-7 engine rated at 1,200 horsepower. Armament consisted of a 20 mm cannon firing through the propeller nose hub, plus two 7.9 mm machine guns mounted in the wings. High altitude performance allowed the Emil to engage the Spitfire on even terms, although the Spitfire is considered to have the edge in outturning the Bf 109.

The Bf 109 G "Gustav," along with the Fw 190, would be there waiting when the Eighth Air Force arrived on the scene. Armament was the same as the Bf 109 Emil, but the Daimler-Benz engine was upgraded to 1,475 HP. Further upgrades to Gustav in both power and armament would follow.

Scramble—That Eternal Summer

CHAPTER 3 THE FEW

It was Winston Churchill who sparked the flame of British resistance, but it was one man – RAF Air Chief Marshal Sir Hugh Dowding – who in 1940 saved Britain from the jaws of Hitler's defense force, the *Wehrmacht*. And 1940 was the year that The Few held Britain together.

Winston Churchill became Britain's Prime Minister on 10 May 1940 as the "Phony War" gave way to a real war. French armed forces were soon in a state of chaos as the Wehrmacht charged virtually unopposed through the Netherlands, Belgium and on into the interior of France. By 26 May, German armored units, the *Panzers*, split the French and British forces and enveloped the right flank of the British army. Some 250,000 men of the British army, virtually trapped on the beachhead at Dunkirk were miraculously evacuated as of 4 June by a diverse flotilla of British craft ranging from destroyers, fishing boats and pleasure craft of every description. The miracle of Dunkirk was a gift of Hitler's decision to let *Reichmarshall* Herman Goering wipe out what was left of the British army's powerless effort to stem the Panzers' advance. Their armament and equipment left behind, the British army was broken, and Britain would soon stand alone, militarily naked in opposing the threat of the invasion soon to follow. Hitler's reasoning for holding the Panzers is unclear, but speculation suggests that he anticipated the end of Churchill's government, and expected his demand that henceforth the British stay out of European affairs would suffice. Churchill, however, thought otherwise.

Dunkirk

If any shred of hope emerged in this crisis – aside from Churchill's fiery speech to fight on – it was a message from the RAF soon delivered to Hitler, Goering, and their Luftwaffe minions. The fight for Dunkirk took place in the skies above the beach areas where the British were trapped during 26 May to 4 June 1940. The Luftwaffe showed up with Messerscmitt Bf 110s and Ju 87 Stukas, escorted by Bf 109s. The Bf 110 was Goering's ace in the hole – the *Zerstoerer* (destroyer) – a twin-engine escort fighter with four machine guns and two 20mm cannons in the nose. It was formidable as a ground support weapon, but underpowered and vulnerable against a Spitfire or Hurricane. Goering had high hopes for the Bf 110 and invested heavily in its numbers, and it was well suited to the task in hand. The Bf 110 also served the Luftwaffe well as a night fighter as the RAF bombing effort unfolded.

The RAF engaged the German air attacks on the British beachhead with fighters mostly from Number 11 Group, deployed in southeast England. The ensuing engagement became a wild dogfight. Albeit without a clear victor, significant lessons were learned by both sides. While the outcome posed no clear winner, it signaled an air battle on near equal terms, even though the RAF was outnumbered. The significant lesson for Goering from the skies above Dunkirk was that the British could and would fight. A second defining moment for Goering and Hitler was learning that the RAF would not be a pushover. Luftwaffe fighter pilots would learn that the Hurricane and Spitfire could out turn the Bf 109, a fundamental performance requirement in aerial combat between fighters. But the Hurricane did not fare well above 15,000 feet. The early Hurricane's Merlin engine had single stage superchargers that limited its performance. The Hurricane, being the "work horse" of the RAF during the Battle of Britain, did very well against the earlier Bf 109 Emil. Early Spitfires (Baby Spits) also had single stage supercharger Merlins, but later production, such as the Spit's MkV upwards and then up to the XIII and IX, had the later Merlin with the two stage supercharger giving it superb high altitude performance.

Among the lessons, the vulnerability of the German Ju 87 *Stuka* (dive bombers) also surfaced. Although accurate as a dive bomber, the Ju 87 would prove to be vulnerable to both Spitfires and Hurricanes as the Battle of Britain evolved. The early engagements also revealed that the RAF formation tactics were clumsy and needed revision. RAF squadron formations consisted of a gaggle of 12 aircraft stacked into four "vics" – three aircraft in a "V" formation, a lead and two wingmen. Only the squadron leader had a panoramic view of the aerial battlefield since the trailing vic pilots were busy flying with eyes glued on the wing tips of their vic leader. Any distraction from that eye concentration could be fatal, and often was. Formations were held together until a vic was dispatched to attack whatever object chosen by the squadron leader, decided with a resounding "Tally Ho." In contrast, Luftwaffe fighter pilots flew a loose "finger four" with the wingman of both pairs guarding the tails of the attacker – tactics that evolved in Spain.

May 16, 1940 – just days after Churchill took the reins of government, the Netherlands and Belgium were already out of the war, and French Premier Paul Reynaud had already accepted the prospects of defeat in a phone call to Churchill on 16 May, as the Wehrmacht poured into France. In the aftermath of Dunkirk, the leaders of France, Great Britain, and Belgium, particularly Reynaud, would be begging for Hurricanes. Reynaud already had 10 Hurricane squadrons deployed on grass fields in France. What any of them thought the Hurricane could do against a tank with its eight 30 caliber machine guns stretches the imagination – tantamount to going after a mad bull with a feather duster. The 10 Hurricane squadrons already in France were committed daily to stopping on-going waves of German bombers escorted by fighters. The RAF commander in France reported that his squadrons were being destroyed in daily combat with superior numbers, and his pilots were worn out with the burden of four or five sorties a day. Reynaud asked Churchill for 10 more, to the consternation of

Hugh Dowding, who insisted that a minimum of 52 squadrons were required for defense of Britain, while he had only 39. The War Cabinet authorized the immediate dispatch of six squadrons to France, later reduced to four with Churchill still pressing for 10, but by 15 May events had overtaken the issue, as French resistance collapsed. The significance of this confusing game of numbers lies in Dowding's short future with the RAF. His personality was crusty at best – argumentative and unyielding. He had many enemies – including then- Chief of the Air Staff Sir Cyril Newall – who were advanced in rank over him. His insistence on attending the War Cabinet meeting on 15 May where he made his case contradicted Churchill's and the War Cabinet's decisions on force structure and sending additional Hurricane squadrons to France. It turned out that Dowding was right, but it also hastened the end of his RAF career that Autumn. Dowding's tenure as the head of Fighter Command and his pending retirement had already been extended to 15 July. As the battle progressed, Dowding's retirement would be extended again to October. Ironically, his departure in mid-October coincided with what is generally regarded as the end of the Battle of Britain.

Unternehmen Seeloeven (Operation Sea Lion)

The setting in late May 1940 is a contrast of euphoric German victory and humiliating British defeat, capped by the fall of France and pending threats of the invasion of England – now standing alone as the last bastion of freedom. Hitler was well into the planning phase of an invasion of England, but apparently Hitler blinked (he will blink again as will be seen subsequently); he at least succumbed to ambivalence as to when to strike. Perhaps it was more a conundrum – the unanswerable question. Goering was calling the shots on the bombing strategy, but Hitler's shadow falls over the setting – invasion or hoax. In Directive No. 16, Hitler ordered preparations for the invasion to be known as *Unternehmen*

Seeloeven – Operation Sea Lion. There is much speculation that he was content to live with a Britain that would remove itself completely from European affairs; in this case, the invasion, fraught with the dangers posed by the turbulent English Channel, the Royal Navy and the RAF, could be unnecessary. Crossing the Channel in towed river barges bearing 250,000 men and 40 thousand horses for their artillery would be no piece of cake. Toss in the resistance and it's little wonder there was ambivalence. There was also a weather window that was critical in the decision-making – May through September. Crossing the water gap between the Belgian and English coasts would have to take place no later than mid-October. Eisenhower knew this in planning for D-Day. Anyone who has sailed between Calais and Dover in winter months would understand how Hitler's barge-borne army might fare in rough seas. Bear in mind that Hitler's Wehrmacht had no designed landing craft to put troops and equipment ashore. The invasion fleet consisted of some 2,400 river barges, only 800 of which had internal power; the rest had to be towed. In any case, Hitler knew that he would have to take out the RAF to succeed. Hitler had already been warned by Admiral Raeder, commander of the *Kriegsmarine* (German Navy), on the weather issue and his assessment that the Navy's support would be limited due to German losses in the Norway invasion. Both General Franz Halder, German Army Chief of Staff, and Alfred Jodl, Chief of the Operations Staff of the Armed Forces (OKW), had serious reservations about the possibility of success.

Adlerangriff (Eagle Offensive)

Plans for the air effort aimed at taking out the RAF before the launch of the British invasion were called *Adlerangriff* (Eagle Offensive), and as such, began to unfold in earnest as the singular objective in German strategy. Dowding's strategy, however, was to buy time, to keep the RAF alive and involve the Luftwaffe in a battle of attrition that would hold off the expected invasion through the end of the weather window of opportunity. Dowding would at the same time carefully husband his defensive assets, misleading the Luftwaffe of England's true strength. Tactically, he would engage the Luftwaffe attacks with an integrated system of command and control fed by the radars of the Chain Home System, the first radar-based air defense system. Through the extraordinary foresight of radio researcher Sir Robert Watson-Watt, the British had in place in 1940 an entire network of long-range early-warning radar stations whose reports were tightly integrated by Fighter Command. Dowding would choose when and how to engage while maintaining a coherent force.

German Order of Battle – July 1940		
Military Group	**Commander**	**Area of Coverage**
Luftwaffe	Herman Goering, Reichmarshall	Luftwaffe Deployment
Luftflotten 2 (Air Fleet)	Arthur Kesserling, Generalfeldmarschall	Southeast England and London
Luftflotten 3 (Air Fleet)	Hugo Sperle, Generalfeldmarschall	Wales and the Midlands
Luftflotten 5 (Air Fleet)	Hans-Jurgen Stumpff, Generalfeldmarschall	Northern England and Scotland

German Aircraft Type	Description
Heinkel He 111 Primary Medium Bomber Medium Altitude	All three had limited payload and range, thus deployed in coastal regions of Belgium, the Netherlands, and France. All three would suffer heavy losses.
Junkers Ju 88 Bomber Medium Range/Altitude	
Dornier Do 17 Bomber Medium Range/Altitude	
Junkers Ju 87 Stuka Dive Bomber	Accurate dive-bomber, but slow and vulnerable ultimately withdrawn from battle by Goering.
Messerschmitt Bf 109 Fighter Limited range level	Armed with two 30 caliber machine guns and two 20 mm canons. Limited range a critical factor.
Messerschmitt Bf 110 Heavy/Night Fighter Used extensively as fighter-bomber and later as radar equipped night fighter	Armed with four 30 cal machine guns and two 20 mm canons in the nose. Lack of maneuverability and acceleration could not match the combat performance of the Spitfire or Hurricane.

United Kingdom Order of Battle – July 1940

Military Group	Commander	Area of Coverage
RAF Fighter Command	Air Chief Marshal Hugh Dowding	Deployed in Sectors

No. 10 Group	Air Vice Marshal Quintin Brand	Southwest England and Wales
No. 11 Group*	Air Vice Marshal Keith Park	Southeast England and London
No. 12 Group	Air Vice Marshal Trafford Leigh-Mallory	The Midlands
No. 13 Group	Air Vice Marshal Richard Saul	Northern England and Scotland

* Note: This Group was strongest, since Dowding anticipated these areas would bear the brunt of the attack.

United Kingdom Aircraft Fighters	Description
Supermarine Spitfire	Armed with six 30 cal machine guns; nimble and fast. Would go after the Bf 109s.
Hawker Hurricane	Armed with eight 30 cal machine guns. Limited performance above 16,000 feet. Tactical use best against bombers, usually operating at that altitude

Following Dunkirk and the demise of France, Germany began to implement the basic strategy of assuring air supremacy over Southeast England in preparation for the invasion. The Luftwaffe began moving two Luftflotten (Air Fleets) into forward airfields in Belgium, the Netherlands, Luxembourg, and Normandy. Luftflotten 2 in the Pas-de-Calais area under General Kesserling was to cover Southeast England and London; Luftflotten 3, further inland in the Orleans/Tours area, commanded by General Sperle, was to cover Wales and the Midlands. Luftflotten 5 under General Stumpf was positioned in Norway to facilitate attacks on northern England and Scotland. This was a huge deployment effort involving the preparation of airfields and the logistics involved in making them operational. Credit is due to the Luftwaffe controllers for the planning and execution of deployment, complete by July 1940 when offensive operations by the Luftwaffe began. Dowding, in the interim between Dunkirk and 15 May, was confronted by the problem of replacing the 453 fighters lost in combat and accidents. Future fighter production would mitigate these losses.

Chain Home Radar System

July 1940 – Initial Luftwaffe attacks marking the opening of the coming battle were aimed at British coastal shipping and ports such as Portsmouth. For context, consider coal as a vital commodity needed to fuel the furnaces of British industry. Sporadic attacks by Ju 87s escorted by Bf 109s went after coal convoys and escorting destroyers. Dowding committed minimal fighter protection, husbanding his fighters for the main event he knew would soon come. Of far more concern to Dowding was the onset of Ju 87 dive-bomber attacks on radar towers of the Chain Home System. The Germans were well aware of the existence of British radar and were well into radar development for their own purposes. What they did not fully understand was that the radar towers stretching along the coastal areas from the English Channel to Scotland were part of an integrated system designed by Dowding for early warning and guiding RAF fighters to the intercept, thereby obviating the need for fuel and time consuming patrols. Dowding correctly anticipated that the full weight of Luftwaffe attacks would come from airfields in Belgium and France, as Luftwaffen 2 and 3 were now deployed in those countries, with Luftwaffen 5 in Norway poised to strike targets in northern England and Scotland. And they would come, like an airborne Golden Horde from the East, with the objective of taking the RAF out of the arena before the invasion.

The radar complex girding the East Coast had the capability of detecting attacking formations, their numbers of aircraft and their direction. They were not yet able to accurately detect altitude. Data inputs were sent to the Fighter Controller at Fighter Command Headquarters, Bentley Priory, where they were plotted on a huge horizontal map by women of the Women's Auxiliary Air Force WAAF (a Dowding innovation), who would prove themselves both capable and courageous in the ensuing months. Many of these women worked in sector control rooms housed in above-ground buildings, such as those at London Biggin Hill Airport, much of which was destroyed by a stray bomb. They stood their ground under fire, and there were casualties. Like the American women who ferried U.S. military aircraft during WW II, they have never been fully recognized.

Data sets were sent from Bentley Park to the operations rooms of 11 and 12 Fighter Group areas where the information was "filtered" and collated. From there, filtered data went to sector airfields where squadrons were "scrambled" and vectored by controllers (again including women) to the intercept – all this action in near "real time" using telephone lines and radio communication with the intercepting aircraft. Telephone links between ground control points were set in concrete underground, another of Dowding's innovations.

Dowding's strength by the end of June 1940 included about 700 fighters and 1,300 fighter pilots organized into the four groups noted earlier. The defensive posture included ground observers, 1,400 wire trailing "sausage" balloons, 4,000 searchlights and 2,000 anti-aircraft guns. These elements were part of the integrated system of defense complemented by the radar-based command

24

and control system.

August to mid-September1940 was the pivotal period for the RAF in the battle. Indeed, a single event on 16 August and other inadvertent attacks on London would turn German strategy to focus on English cities, principally on the city of London.

Adlertag (Eagle Day)

For the Germans it was Adlerangriff (Eagle Offensive) that signaled the beginning of the campaign to gain air supremacy over the invasion landing areas. The main attack was called *Adlertag* (Eagle Day). After several delays due to bad weather, Adlertag was reset for 13 August 1940. There was little activity until 8 August when Channel convoys were attacked by Ju 87s escorted by Bf 109s. The Luftwaffe lost 31 aircraft to the RAF's 19 and had a graphic awakening that the Ju 87 was no match for British fighters. On 11 August there was a large engagement over the Channel involving fighters – the score essentially a draw: 38 German to 32 British.

A rehearsal for Adlertag took place on 12 August. Attacks were aimed at RAF coastal airfields and radar installations with very little positive effect. One Luftwaffe objective was to lessen the numbers of British fighters available on Adlertag. The RAF lost 22; the Luftwaffe 31.

Goering attempted to launch the full weight of Luftflotten 2 and 3 on 13 August. The attacking force consisted of 197 Ju 87s and Ju 88s escorted by Bf 109s. Adlertag got off to a shaky start due to faulty weather assessments by German meteorologists. As a result, a recall was issued to halt morning operations. Some of the attacking units did not get the recall message and went on to their targets. Eleven RAF airfields were bombed as well as a raid on Southampton that leveled a bicycle factory, a furniture storage warehouse and a meat depot – a spurious selection of targets due to faulty intelligence, and certainly nothing of military value. The Vickers-Supermarine factory was overlooked. Typically, there were wild claims on both sides, but the RAF lost 13 fighters. After the engagement, the Luftwaffe concluded Dowding was down to between 200 and 300 fighters – just what he wanted them to conclude. Part of his strategy was to mislead the Luftwaffe on England's actual strength to keep the battle alive until after the acceptable Channel weather window closed, and to bleed the Luftwaffe to death in the interim.

On August 14, piecemeal Luftwaffe attacks continued throughout the day. Eleven RAF bases were bombed. The RAF lost 8 aircraft, the Luftwaffe 19. Ju 87s participating in the attacks took a fearful beating, and they were soon withdrawn from the battle scene by Goering due to unacceptable attrition.

The German plan for August 15 was the grand assault – to throw the full weight of all three Luftwaffen into the arena simultaneously. It would turn out to be the biggest air battle to date. Luftwaffen 5 would go after targets in Northern England while Luftwaffen 2 and 3 would attack Fighter Command airfields in the south. The idea was to limit RAF fighter support to Group 11 (Southeast England and London) from Groups 12 and 13 (the Midlands and Northern England and Scotland). Such support from Group 12 had not yet been the case, and Group 13 was too far north. Luftflotten 5 attacks from Norway consisted of 65 He 111s escorted by 34 B4 110s. Both took a pasting from Group 13 defenders. From Denmark, 50 Ju 88s were launched without escort. Airfields were attacked with minimal results at a cost of 24 German aircraft shot down. The RAF lost none. In the south, however, German bombers had a significant number of Bf 109s to support them. RAF airfields in southern England came under attack, and the weight of the attack caused significant concern as well as damage to several key airfields, putting defending RAF fighter pilots in a multi-sortie situation – fly, fight, land and refuel, and take off again in near exhaustion. By the end of the day, the RAF shot down 75 German aircraft at a cost of 34. The Luftwaffe could have achieved a coup had they found a way to catch refueling RAF fighters on the ground.

Bombs Fall On London

Events that took place on August 15 had particular significance on the outcome of the battle and would lead to a change in German strategy, as well as the Blitz on London and other English cities. *Hauptmann* (Group Leader) Walter Robensdoerffer, leading a Epro 210 group specializing in precision, low level attacks, lost his way approaching RAF Kenley, his intended target, and inadvertently bombed Croydon, London's prime civilian airport. Unfortunately for Robensdoerffer and the Luftwaffe, Croydon was within London's city limits and very much the wrong target to bomb. Hitler had specifically called London targets off limits, meaning that only he had the authority to order such an attack. Hitler's reasoning is said to relate to some vague notion that he still harbored the idea of peacefully working a deal with Churchill and avoiding the exchange of bombing raids on the two capital cities. Hitler issued appropriate orders that had gone down the Luftwaffe chain of command. No matter to Hauptmann Robensdoerffer, who would die before the guns of a Group 11 fighter, thus avoiding the wrath of the incensed Hitler. Other "inadvertent" attacks on London would follow, leading to Churchill's token raid on Berlin on 26 August 1940. In turn, Hitler's reply was to unleash the blitzkrieg "lightening war," at the same time putting the RAF in a recovery mode.

Goering Blinks

Goering, far from observing the battle scene from his perch on the

French coast, was in conference with his staff at *Karinhall*, his country estate in Germany. Along with his Luftflotten commanders were two of his top fighter pilots: Adolph Galland who, would lead the Luftwaffe Fighter Command, and Werner Moelders, its leading ace. Goering had persuaded himself to believe that his fighter escort pilots were busy seeking glory in their engagements with the RAF, rather than doing their primary job of protecting the bombers. He therefore directed that escort fighters fly wing-to-wing with the bomber formations. To no avail, both Galland and Moelders tried to reason with Goering, pointing out that the rigid change would rob the escorts of their main tactical advantage – altitude. Also lost would be their ability to catch defending fighters as they rose in defense. For the short range Bf 109, fuel consumption in this environment would limit their fighting time. Himself a fighter pilot from WW I, Goering's reasoning defies understanding; then again, he was not flying a Bf 109 in combat. The lesson would not be lost on Doolittle in the spring of 1944, who turned his escort P-51s "loose" when the P-51 entered the fray.

The Hardest Day

August 18 – the British refer to it as "the hardest day." It makes more sense in this author's mind to call it an aerial Armageddon – overshadowing even August 15th and in many ways foreshadowing things to come – but nothing as yet in the Battle of Britain would match the length and sheer intensity of the engagement on 18 August. The German objective was to take out Biggin Hill and Kenley, both RAF sector airfields in key defensive positions, in the approaches to London in the event of an invasion. Both airfields had operations control rooms above ground where "filtered" information made its way to the sector control rooms along the control chain discussed earlier. What puzzles this author is the fact that the German intelligence – while it recognized the radar chain as the "eyes of the RAF," it apparently did not penetrate the system to the point that it understood how the data were used in controlling fighter defensive tactics. Above ground control rooms were not singled out nor targeted; had they been taken out in major attacks on RAF airfields, the results may have been very different.

German planning for the Luftflotten 2 attack was impeccable. Strikes were to be layered attacks in terms of altitude and timing. The planned raids on Biggin Hill and Kenley by He 111s, Do 17s and Ju 88s were to be simultaneous. Fighter sweeps in this case were set to detract the defensive fighters from the targets. The He 111s would attack Biggin Hill from high altitude. At the same time, Kenley would undergo high altitude and dive-bombing attacks, and finally an attack on the deck to destroy remnants of the airfield infrastructure. The attacking force consisted of 108 bombers and 150 fighters.

A superb plan no doubt; unfortunately for the Luftwaffe, execution was anything but. Nine RAF squadrons were waiting for them. Keith Park's Group 11 also had three squadrons in reserve and six more if needed from No.10 Group. Breakdowns in timing and assembly were such that the brilliant plan became a disjointed mess. Dornier (Do) 17s led by Hauptmann Joachim Roth, supposed to be the last clean up effort at Kenley, were instead the first. They approached the White Cliffs on the deck to avoid radar detection, but were picked up by ground observers deployed on the coast and flew through a blizzard of ground fire thereafter. Roth would lose nearly half of his strike force. He was brought down among them but survived. The high altitude force was attacking Kenley, but not as planned. Ju 88 dive-bombers were out of phase arriving with Kenley already burning. Damage to Kenley was extensive with many homes nearby hit by stray bombs, but the airfield was back in operation within a few hours. The high altitude attack on Biggin Hill had even less successful. Most of the bombs fell in woods and open fields surrounding the airfield.

As the survivors of Luftflotten 2 were returning to their bases with what their leaders regarded as great success, Luftflotten 3 aircraft were leaving theirs to attack Portsmouth and surrounding islands including the Isle of Wight, with the largest number of Ju 87s ever assembled for a single raid. They were escorted by 157 fighters. The Ju 87, soon to be withdrawn from the battle scene, had already demonstrated that it was easy meat for the likes of a Spitfire or Hurricane. The attack was also launched out of phase with those on Biggin Hill and Kenley. The bases to be attacked were Royal Navy – not RAF. Sixteen Stukas were shot down as were eight Bf 109s, with a loss of only five British fighters. So much for brilliant planning.

Late in the afternoon of 18 August, Luftflotten 2 struck again, this time flying up the Thames estuary to attack RAF fighter units at Croydon, apparently no longer off limits; Manston station, northeast of Kent, was attacked by fighters.

With both sides licking their wounds, the day cost the RAF 27 fighters with 10 pilots killed. The Luftwaffe lost 71 aircraft, with 94 killed and 24 captured. The cost was high – as high as it got to this point in time – but mostly to the Luftwaffe. Combined aircraft and crew losses this day were higher than any other engagement during the campaign – including the aerial battle on 15 September now celebrated as the Battle of Britain Day. Even if one counts that surviving German crewmen shot down over England were out of the war, that was not the case for RAF pilots sharing the experience. Consider also that the Luftwaffe, while bearing the enormous cost of the operation, had hardly made a dent in the RAF infrastructure, its aircraft or its available pilots. Hardest day indeed for aircrews; for Londoners there would be even harder days – and nights – ahead.

One glaring flaw in the defensive posture of the RAF was the lack of coordination and support between Groups 11 (Park) and 12

(Leigh-Mallory). Relations between the two were tenuous at best, contentious at worst. There were two issues: Group 11 bore the brunt of Luftwaffe attacks approaching southeast England from bases along the Belgium and French coastal areas. The weight of these attacks could often overtax Park's resources, requiring support from Groups 10 (west) and 12 (to Park's north). August 18 is a case in point. Support from Leigh-Mallory was anything but robust – call it token. Group 12 airmen were apparently convinced that Group 11 was reaping all the glory.

The Big Wing

Among Fighter Command defense issues was tactics – rooted in the "big wing" concept offered by Leigh-Mallory as an improved alternative for dealing with incoming bomber formations. Leigh-Mallory was supported avidly in agitating for the adoption of the tactic by the renowned fighter ace Douglas Bader. Basically, the concept called for scrambling three squadrons that would join in formation in preparation for the intercept, bringing to bear much greater strength than a single squadron. Neither Dowding nor Park agreed with the idea and resisted the change. Their view was that it would take too much time to assemble the three squadrons, as well as concern about how the assembled squadrons would work with ground controllers. To this author, also a pilot who has flown time-consuming formation assembly, it recalls the issue of the 12-aircraft RAF squadron that surfaced over Dunkirk, with only one pilot with a view of the battle field and the other 11 with eyes fixed on the wingtips of another aircraft. The RAF went through this awakening over Dunkirk and thereby adopted the "finger four" formation used by the Luftwaffe as an alternative. This prompts the question: how would the individual defending fighters be fed into the battle? Interestingly, the big wing idea was later put to work with some success against German daylight attacks on the city of London.

August 19 – 23, 1940 brought night raids on English cities, as well as Glasgow and Edinburgh, providing a good demonstration of what the Luftwaffe could do with its radar navigation system called *Knickebein*, in which radio beams were projected in crossing radials to give both bearing and range signals. Aircrews flew along one radial – a bearing orientated to the target. Their payloads were released when intersecting the crossing range signal, also intersecting the target. The system was useful for night operations and accurate enough to position the aircraft over an intended target area. Despite that capability, German bombs would still find ways to be where they shouldn't, with random drops from damaged or lost aircraft. The RAF would develop similar "blind bombing" targeting systems – initially Gee and subsequently Oboe.

Churchill Returns The Favor

On the night of 24 – 25 August 1940, London was heavily bombed, this time by bombers of Sperle's Luftflotten 3 and due to another navigation error. Churchill, then unaware of such mitigating circumstances, was nonetheless enraged by the event and now in a retaliatory frame of mind, and as a result sent 75 Wellingtons and Hampdens to attack Berlin that night – a place which had before been ostensibly considered an industrial target. These Luftwaffe attacks on London with responsive raids on Berlin by the RAF not only set off the catastrophic Blitz on London, but also set the path for the destruction of Cologne, Hamburg, Berlin, Dresden, and other German cities by the RAF. Ironically, and critical to Dowding, this new thrust on cities provided the breathing space he needed for the RAF's survival.

German Stukas were now gone from scene, and Bf 110s' operations were curtailed so that they could be escorted by Bf 109s. It was also decided to reorder strategic thinking to again focus attacks on RAF airfields and factories that were producing

Spitfires and Hurricanes. Fighter Command would now be put on a negative curve of aircraft and pilot strength as the fighting dragged on. Several historians suggest the outlook for the RAF was bordering on dangerous. In *The Narrow Margin*, authors Derek Wood and Derek Dempster relate that in the two weeks from 24 August to 6 September, 295 British fighter planes were totally destroyed and 171 badly damaged, compared to a total output of 269 new and repaired Spitfires and Hurricanes. Also, 103 pilots were killed or missing and 128 were wounded, which represented a total of 120 pilots per week out of a fighting strength of just fewer than 1,000. During August no more than 260 fighter pilots were trained, and casualties in the same month were just over 300. A full squadron complement was 26 pilots; the average in August was 16. In their assessment, the RAF was losing the battle. Denis Richards, in his 1953 contribution to the official British account of *History of the Second World War*, agreed that lack of pilots, especially experienced ones, was the RAF's greatest problem. Three more weeks at such a pace would have exhausted aircraft reserves. On 7 September RAF aircraft losses fell below British production and remained so until the end of the war.

Adolph Galland was hardly any better off; he never had more than 1,000 to 1,200 fighter pilots. Regarding the cost of the battle in terms of human life, we tend to overlook the death rate among young German airmen, hardly the fire-breathing Nazis seen in propaganda visuals. Rather, most were young loyal products of the Fatherland, equally courageous in continuing to fly and fight in what most already knew was a lost cause. Based on my own wartime experience, I am often curious about mind-sets of combatants on both sides. It brings to mind the following statement in Donald Miller's outstanding book, *Masters of the Air*, as written by radio operator J.J. Lynch of the U.S. Eighth Air Force: "we live in fear but not for a consuming hatred for another human, who given his wish, would not be involved in this madness any more than we."

August 26 – the Luftwaffe returned to Kenley and Biggin Hill in the daylight and that night attacked industrial targets. Forty-one German aircraft went down; the British lost 28 fighters. Dowding was now eating into his reserves. Based on continuing losses at that level, his reserves would be exhausted in three weeks. Losing pilots was the more critical outlook.

For the balance of August 1940, German raids continued with night bombing of British industrial cities: Portsmouth, Liverpool and Birmingham among them. The Birmingham raid hit the Spitfire factory at Castle Bromwich and other production facilities. Day raids continued on Group 11 airfields, mainly Biggin Hill that was put out of operation temporarily twice with heavy casualties – 39 killed on the ground with 26 wounded.

August 31 – Fighter Command lost 39 aircraft and 14 pilots; the Germans lost 41 aircraft. The unrelenting waves of attacking bombers were now a matter of deep concern, especially the loss of experienced pilots. Losses were such that squadron strength, normally 26 pilots was depleted. Sheer pilot exhaustion by the repetition of daily sorties they were required to fly was a significant problem, yet they flew, and continued to fly until relieved or dead.

On the first of September, 450 German aircraft hit airfields and destroyed the sector control room at Biggin Hill. These raids continued through 6 September with Fighter Command beginning to fold under the pressure. So close to the end, a surprising thing happened. In stepped Hitler, who with Goering on 7 September made the decision to shift from British airfields and factories to bombing London and other cities. *Seeloerven* (Sea Lion) was now reset for 21 September, but too late in the weather window for a secure operation. Yet it remained on the table for the time being. It would soon fade away like an old soldier.

Blitzkrieg

With bombs falling on the city of London, the *blitzkrieg* genie was now out of the bottle. Attacks on London began in earnest 7 September 1940 taking the lives of 412 Londoners – again on 9 September, 370 were killed. On 11 September, 500 Luftwaffe bombers attacked London, Portsmouth and Southampton by daylight; 200 more that night hit London again and Liverpool. The shift in German targeting was now apparent. The Blitz was on.

September 12 – 14 attacks continued, but on a lesser scale due to weather and Luftwaffe changes in strategy toward more frequent but smaller raids. Daylight bombing of London by the Luftwaffe brought the full weight of Dowding's Fighter Command into the defensive mix. The earlier defensive scheme had Park's Group 11 going after the bombers with Groups 10 and 12 covering his airfields. With the huge Luftwaffe bomber formations now targeting London, all three RAF Groups were brought up to stop them. Some German planes got through, but the bomber formations were scattered, as were their bombs. Under the heavy pressure brought to bear, many German bombers aborted the mission and returned to their bases In France and Belgium.

Hitler "Postpones" The Invasion

September 15 was a day of high hopes for the Luftwaffe – perfect weather and a key day in the Battle of Britain. Goering was again poised for the *coup de grace*. Luftwaffe attacks were planned for both the morning, with 250 aircraft, and 600 more in the afternoon. Group Captain Bader's "big wing" would have time to form up for the defense. Group 11 had sixteen squadrons with five more from Group 12 to confront the Germans. The Luftwaffe formations were under attack from the coastal point of entry to the London area. The RAF fighter defense was such that the German formations began to break up. Nonetheless, as expected, some

35

bombers got through to hit sections of London with random destruction, but nothing apt to bring London to its knees, as Goering had hoped would happen. In the afternoon, Park's Group 11 fighters refueled and re-armed and were ready and waiting – if they had not been, the Luftwaffe could have dealt a crippling blow. Incoming bomber formations under attack were again scattered, dropping their bombs randomly in London's suburbs. One German formation was turned back in disorder after suffering heavy losses. The German assault was smashed at a cost of 60 aircraft; while the RAF lost 26 Hurricanes and Spitfires. September 15 did not end the war, but it does mark a date of decisive victory. Two days later – September 17 – Hitler ordered the postponement of the operation, also ordering the dispersal of the invasion fleet in order to avert further damage by British air and naval attacks.

The bombing of London continued throughout September with the objective of destroying its infrastructure and terrorizing its citizenry. Londoners were not intimidated as expected, but rather infused with resolve to resist. The irony is also apparent. The shift of German strategy to London and other British cities rather on RAF airfields and aircraft production was the reprieve the RAF needed to recover and rebuild.

The Battle Of Britain Ends

Given the "postponement" of the invasion (that would fade away in a natural death), 15 September is recognized in the UK as the end of the Battle of Britain, the first of significant turn-around victories for Britain and an enormous morale builder for the British people. The cost in terms of human life was also enormous. The Battle of Britain Memorial at Capel-le-Ferne overlooking the White Cliffs lists 2,946 names of those RAF pilots who flew; 537 were killed. Civilian casualties, July through December 1940 were 23,000 dead and 32,138 wounded, an indication of what would lay ahead with the Blitz. London casualties were some 50,000 dead overshadowing all those for the rest of England. As we shall see in succeeding chapters, these numbers add to the enormity of death from the air elsewhere, in Warsaw, Rotterdam, Cologne, Hamburg, Dresden and the other cities of Germany laid in waste by the combined weight of the RAF and the U.S. Army Air Force.

But it was "the few" who saved Britain, and they are commemorated name by name in stone at Capel-le-Ferne. Winston Churchill summed it all up: "Never in the field of human conflict was so much owed by so many to so few." Pilots who fought in the Battle have been known as *The Few* ever since.

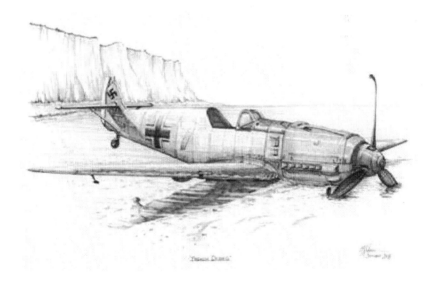

BF 109 Down

Against All The Odds

Don't Just Stand There—Get One Up

In Quick—Punch Hard—Get Out

Costal Defenders

Salute to the Few

A Tough Tour Completed

41

CHAPTER 4   THE MANY: RAF Bomber Command

Readiness for war as it approached in 1939 was not Britain's strong suit, but rather a negative military posture in relation to German power, especially the case for the RAF. When the war began in September 1939, the RAF had 536 bombers and 608 fighters compared to the Luftwaffe strength of 2,130 bombers and 1,215 fighters. Workhorse aircraft comprising RAF Bomber Commands' strike force were the Vickers Wellington, Armstrong Whitworth Whitley, Handley Page Hampden and the Fairey Battle. These were all twin-engine medium bombers except for the single engine Battle. Both range and capacities were totally unsuited for an extensive strategic bombing effort against Germany. Bomber Command was, however, moving forward with developing new four engine aircraft with payload capacity and range to hit targets deep in Germany. The Handley Page Halifax, Short Sterling and the superb Avro Lancaster, were all in production, with the Lancaster, to my mind WW2's most capable bombing platform until the U.S. Army Air Force B-29 made its appearance in 1944. These British "heavies" all had the requisite performance capabilities; what they lacked initially were sub-systems for navigation in locating targets to satisfactorily exploit these capabilities.

Early bombing operations had RAF Bomber Command on a costly learning curve. Twin-engine aircraft were sent forth on sorties to mine German river mouths and drop propaganda leaflets, while fear of launching attacks on populated areas that might engender war crimes constrained operations. For example, a force of 149 twin-engine Wellingtons was dispatched on 18 December 1939 for a daylight raid on the German Baltic port of Wilhelmshaven. The Wellingtons were taken on by Luftwaffe fighters that had been guided to the intercept, in itself a surprise for the RAF, since they were unaware of the Luftwaffe's use of radar or even its existence. The Wellingtons made their way to Wilhelmshaven locating two German naval ships, but never dropped a bomb. The concern: had they missed the ships and killed German civilians in the target area, they could have faced courts martial on return to base. The Wellingtons exited the target now enveloped in flak only to be set upon by German fighters. Half of the attacking force fell before German guns; three more in crash landings at their home base. Do the bombers always get through? Some perhaps always, but not all. The lesson – 60 percent loss rate – was unacceptable, and as a result, daylight operations were switched to night.

Bomber Command was on a growth curve propelled by the thinking of Air Marshal "Boom" Trenchard and members of the Air Council who were dedicated to the concept of strategic bombing as the road to victory. By December 1940, production of the flawed twin engine Manchester finally ended. Of the 200 ordered, 157 were delivered as Manchesters, the remaining 43 were four engine Lancasters – originally designated as Manchester IIIs.

With production of capable aircraft now flowing and training of aircrews well advanced, losses of aircraft and crews were growing unabated. By September 1940, with the war now through its first year, the RAF lost 1,908 aircrew, and that number more than doubled to 4,330 the next year. In 1942, casualties nearly doubled again to 8,018; nor would the bloody toll stop there.

Despite the losses, in the minds of Churchill, the Air Council, Trenchard and the Air Staff, the application of growing strike capability was largely driven by strategy. The seeds of such thinking had stemmed from the idea of going after the cities – destroying an enemy's ability to create the implements of war and to intimidate their populations. The coupling of these ideas was very much on the table of discussion. The events that propelled British thinking and conduct fell out of the Blitzkrieg. On 7 September 1940, 365 Luftwaffe bombers attacked the Port of London in the daylight with bombs that also fell in residential areas. Attacks continued that night. Over 400 Londoners died. London was attacked almost nightly with both high explosive and incendiary bombs between mid-September and mid-November. What the British call "The Second Great Fire of London" took place on 29 December 1940, when the Luftwaffe attacked the city of London with both fire and high explosive bombs. Results were devastating. Arthur Harris, who would rise to lead Bomber Command, witnessed the fire storm. Other cities in England were subjected to the same savagery. By the end of May 1940, 43,000 people had been killed in English cities – to say nothing of the extensive destruction of property. It does not take much imagination to consider the reactive mind-sets of British people and their leaders.

Throughout this period of destruction until 22 February 1942, Bomber Command was led by Air Chief Marshal Sir Richard Peirse. When he took command, he had 34 squadrons of twin-engine bombers of limited performance for deep sorties. When he left, he had 48 squadrons of legitimate "heavies" – three of Stirlings, three of Halifaxes and three of Manchesters. Expansion was on-going with airfield construction and aircrew training to keep pace.

The Butt Study

As the RAF night-bombing effort unfolded over the first two years of operations, it became clear that Bomber Command had no reliable way to assess results other than estimates provided by returning aircrews at debriefings. There was suspicion and some evidence that bombs were being dropped a long way from the intended targets. As a result, by 1941, strike cameras were being fitted to the bombers that were triggered by the bomb release.

Subsequent photo interpretation revealed shocking inaccuracies. English physicist Frederick Lindemann, better known as Lord Cherwell, was a close friend of Churchill. In his capacity as Chief Scientific Advisor to the Cabinet, he appointed a civil servant in the War Cabinet Secretariat named David Bensusan-Butt to assess over 600 photos and compare them to aircrew claims. This was happening on Peirse's watch and cannot have helped his future.

Results of the Butt study were made known on 18 August 1941 and confirmed what had already been suspected:

1. Of those aircraft recorded as attacking their target, only 1 in 3 got within 5 miles.

2. Over the French ports, the proportion was 2 in 3; over Germany as a whole, the proportion was 1 in 4; over the Ruhr Valley it was only 1 in 10.

3. In the full moon, the proportion was 2 in 5; in the new moon it was only 1 in 15.

4. All these figures relate only to aircraft recorded as attacking the target; the proportion of the total sorties which reached within 5 miles is less than one-third.

The conclusion seems to follow that only about one-third of aircraft claiming to reach their target actually reached it.

Winston Churchill was angered by these conclusions but had little recourse but to persevere with the only weapon at his disposal for attacking Germany directly. It was to be "gloves off." Bomber Command was directed to go after German transportation systems and the morale of its civilians. Further, in Cherwell's "de-housing" paper, area bombing of German cities was emphasized to eliminate the labor force.

Air Marshal Sir Arthur Harris took the leadership of Bomber

Command in February 1942. A disciple of Trenchard, who had an unwavering belief that the war could be won by the bomber, Harris pursued this course with steadfast commitment. Bomber Command was directed to target 58 German industrial cities with the objective of terrorizing populations and, in particular, de-housing the labor force. Harris gets a bum rap; he did not formulate such policy, but he did believe that destruction of German cities was the key to interdicting the production of the tools of war.

Deadly skies, it was indeed. The blood-letting in the air continued – in 1942 Bomber Command flew 35,000 sorties and lost 1,716 aircraft at a loss rate of 4.8 percent. On the night of 24 – 25 August it would be 7.1 percent over Frankfurt. Aircrew morale was now a serious problem.

The Wizard War

The obvious operational failures leading to the Butt Report would plant developments that provided solutions to the navigation problem, and also tactics. At this point it's useful to explore a topic that embraced commonality to all three air forces in this narrative: the RAF, the U.S. Army Air Force, and the Luftwaffe. No discussion of the air war in WW II would be complete without addressing the role of electronics – perhaps the mother lode of what bonded the elements of tactics, aircraft, weapons and aircrews into an effective whole.

The explosive evolution of microwave technology in WW II had a profound effect on both the offensive and defensive components of the air war. Movement toward the application of radar principles known even before the war reached an accelerated level on both sides as physicists turned from pure research and began developing electronic systems geared to the demands imposed by the wartime scenario. Evolving technology was directed toward submarine detection and fire control systems for ground and aircraft platforms. Of prime interest here is the war in the air. Focal points of microwave technology application appeared in the United States, Britain and Germany, all with parallel efforts as the war gained momentum.

British intelligence based on analysis of microwave transmissions and Enigma decryption intercepts had already established that the Luftwaffe was using a radio navigation technique in their strikes against targets in the UK during the Battle of Britain. The systems in use provided a beam for direction to the target area and one or more crossing beams to determine the bomb release point. At the time German radars for air defense were not known to the British. However, British intelligence penetrated such developments establishing the existence of the *Freya* early warning radar system (named for a Norse goddess of war), and the much more effective *Wurtzburg* gun-laying radar system. Both were used extensively and effectively in the German air defense scheme.

By the spring of 1942, the RAF abandoned the concept of precision daylight bombing and moved toward a policy of massive area bombing on cities, still aimed at taking out not only factories and facilities within them, but also their labor force. As we have already seen, another motive advocated by Arthur Harris was to terrorize the inhabitants of German cities – oddly enough an idea already disproved by attacks on London and other English cities. Harris should have known better, in the ensuing RAF onslaughts against Cologne and Hamburg and others, German morale did not break any more than that of the British in the air raids on London.

In order to sustain such a bombing offensive, aircraft had to be able to accurately locate their objectives at night regardless of the weather. Radar and radio aids to navigation were now essential to the success of the campaign. Early developments deemed applicable by the RAF were the *Gee* and *Oboe* "blind bombing" navigation systems. Neither of these devices could be considered radar systems since they did not use reflected signals. Gee employed three intersecting sets of timed radio pulses and a receiver in the aircraft that could measure time along the compass bearing of each pulse. Using special maps, the position of the aircraft with respect to the target could be intersected and plotted. Gee was unsuitable for bombing targets 250 miles distant, since accuracy declined with distance. The system employed line of sight transmission of pulses, thus the curvature of the earth limited its useful range. Gee sets were installed in U.S. Eighth Air Force bombers and used effectively for navigation, but not in bombing operations.

Oboe used two ground stations, one referred to as the "cat" and the other the "mouse." Aircraft equipped with Oboe carried a transmitting beacon by which it could be guided by the "cat" to fly a set course and distance that would take over the target. The cat station provided guidance information to the aircraft through an audible signal that sounded like a musical tone, hence the name "oboe." Using the on-board beacon transmitter, the mouse also tracked range information calculating and transmitting the bomb release signal precisely over the target. Oboe was accurate at distances up to 250 miles, but like Gee, accuracy fell off exponentially beyond that range. Although relatively accurate within its effective range, Oboe was not good enough.

The development of an on-board radar system with a cathode ray tube display capable of discerning surface features became the focus of development and the key to the RAF carpet bombing technique used for the rest of the war. The system developed was the *H2S*, so named for "home sweet home" with "home" representing the target. The plan called for H2S-equipped "pathfinder" aircraft to find their way deep into Germany and mark the target area with flares on which aircraft of the main bomber stream would make their drops.

The German response to the onslaught of night and day bomb strikes against their cities was systematic and effective. Their system was especially critical in defense against RAF night attacks. Similar to Dowding's, the German system linked search and detection radar, searchlights, flak batteries, day and night interceptors and control centers in their air defense scheme. Two ground-based radar systems were key components: the *Freya*, which could scan for 100 miles in all directions, and the narrow beam *Wurzburg* that had a range of 36 miles. These radars were set up in zones: one Freya and two Wurzburgs in each. The Freya provided early warning. One Wurzburg tracked the incoming bomber while the other controlled the interceptor. The development of an airborne radar system further enhanced the German defenses against the RAF. The system known as *Lichtenstein SN 2* was installed in the Messerschmitt Bf 110 along with upgraded engines and armament. The aircraft could be directed to the intercept where its four machine guns and two 20-mm cannons could be brought to bear on the invader. The Bf 110, a failure as a twin-engine day fighter, became the premier Luftwaffe night fighter. As the RAF strikes intensified, the German air defense system came into its own in terms of effectiveness.

These same German air defenses were no less effective against the Eighth Bomber Command by tracking incoming formations, vectoring day fighters to the intercept and controlling anti-aircraft fire. Both the RAF and the Eighth Bomber Command would pay heavily in lost aircraft and airmen as the Germans fine-tuned their system.

Jamming techniques, countermeasures and counter-countermeasures raged on through the war's end in Europe in what became known as the "Wizard War." British countermeasure experts developed an airborne jammer code named *Mandrel* that produced an array of electronic noise designed to overwhelm the German Freyas. Another tactic called a spoof was introduced about the same time. Unlike jamming, the spoof device – called *Moonshine* – was designed to deceive the enemy radar without their operators knowing it. Moonshine was triggered by the pulse from a German radar and responded with a wide range of signals on the same wavelength. The effect was to simulate a display indicating a large number of aircraft in tight formation. Meanwhile, physicists in the U.S. were busy developing their own jammers aimed at the Freyas and Wurzburgs.

The introduction of *Window* by the RAF was one of the widely used methods of deceiving German radars. Window was aluminum foil cut in strips of about 25 cm in length and carried by bombers in bundles of one pound packets of several hundred strips each. Known to us as "Chaff," these bundles were dropped from the waist windows by gunners every minute or two when approaching the target area, thus filling the radar screens with false echoes. Germans would eventually counter-chaff by upgrading the Wurzburg with a new system known as *Wurzlaus*. The Wurzlaus was a coherent, pulse Doppler radar that could isolate aircraft from the chaff induced snowfall-like noise that filled the operator's radarscope display.

The range and intensity of the development and application of electronic systems to the war effort on both sides is simply mind boggling to me. Author Robert Buderi described it as the "Wizard's War" and that is the ideal context – a war of minds at war within a war.

The Pathfinders

Group Captain Sydney Bufton, at age 33, was appointed Deputy Director of Bombing Operations at the British Air Ministry and set his mind to the problem of bombing accuracy. At the same time he became a thorn in the side of Arthur Harris by proposing specialized pathfinder squadrons, officially a Target Finding Force

(TFF). These units were to be manned by experienced pilots. Harris saw the proposal as creating elite units, essentially draining away his best aircrews. While Harris strongly opposed the idea, he eventually gave in, and Bufton's proposal was adopted by the formation of a separate No. 8 Group in August 1942. The group comprised four squadrons, and they did indeed become elite with aircrews that coveted the brass albatross below their RAF wings. The TFF would become the PFF – Pathfinder Force. What fell out of all this – metaphorically – was a virtual symphony of execution; finders, illuminators, and markers with a conductor (Master Bomber) orbiting overhead to make sure the players were all in tune with the music.

The twin-engine de Haviland Mosquito with its unique capabilities was particularly well suited to the pathfinder operation. Components of operation included:

- Pathfinders were tasked with dropping illuminating flares along the route to the target to lead the bombers to the appointed target.

- Illuminators were PFF aircraft flying in front of the main force to drop target indicators (TIs).

- Markers would drop incendiaries onto the TIs prior to the arrival of the bomber stream.

- The Master Bomber would circle the target throughout the raid, using radio to guide bombers to burning markers.

Pathfinders flew over 50,000 sorties against targets in German cities at a cost of 3,727 airmen killed in these operations, another high price in human life for the airmen, not to mention the cost in human life for those civilians killed in the target areas.

The development of the Pathfinder Force and the application of these elements of coordination and control made the RAF area bombing strategy a reality with unmitigated success in the fire bombing of so many German cities. They lit the fires on a wide scale, but questions arose as to the success of the process in terms of ending production of key industrial targets, taking out the labor force, or in fact terrorizing the population into submission.

The Casablanca Conference

The Casablanca Conference took place in January 1943, the first war conference among the Allies, and intended to plan the Allied European war strategy for the next phase of the war. Planned as a meeting of the "Big Three" (allies Britain, the United States, and Russia), it in fact evolved as a meeting of the big two, since Joseph Stalin refused to leave Moscow. Air leaders attending for the British included Air Marshal Sir Charles Portal of the Air Ministry, Marshal of the RAF Hugh Trenchard, and Air Chief Marshal Arthur Harris, commander of RAF Bomber Command. Commanding General of the USAAF Hap Arnold, 12th Air Force Commander in North Africa Major General Carl Spaatz, and Eighth Air Force commander Major General Ira Eaker were among the Americans. The focus of the conference was on resolving differences in invasion thrusts – North Africa as proposed by Britain versus the American preference of a direct invasion of Western Europe offered by General George Marshall, U.S. Army Chief of Staff. The conference had an air campaign component that had a profound effect on the evolution of Anglo American strategy. There were significant differences over the paths that bombing operations should take that required resolution. But it was agreed by all – except for Harris – that bombing alone would not win the war.

A side issue involved Eaker, who exploded when Hap Arnold told him the President was under pressure from Churchill to convert from daylight bombing to night operations in concert with the RAF. Eaker responded with the fact that his aircraft were not equipped for night operations, and his crews were not trained for it. Eaker put his case in writing, and when he addressed the leaders directly he not only held his ground but offered a counter proposal for both day operations by the Eighth AF and night bombing by the RAF – this would soon be known as "round the clock" bombing. Churchill relented as did Roosevelt, and it was "Round the Clock" operations that went forward as the air campaign unfolded.

Of major significance in the conference deliberations was the evolution of target selection, and it is here that different paths were taken in the application of Allied strategic air power. Within a framework of general objectives, a new directive called "POINTBLANK" was prepared by the RAF Air Staff that focused on specific industrial targets. The directive was based on the Air Staff's notion that bombing one or more precision targets would be a "panacea" to a quick end of the war. Harris thought not, and held that the whole point of bombing was to destroy German cities and everything in them. The use of the term "panacea targets" as it was by Harris referred to specific industrial targets, tantamount to calling them a cure-all remedy for the targeting scenario.

The conference agenda mapped out the strategy for conducting military operations against Germany with the ultimate invasion of Western Europe as its center point. Tactics, negotiation and debate produced the "Casablanca Declaration" which embraced the doctrine of unconditional surrender, undeniably a statement of the Allies' intent to annihilate Hitler and his minions. While the focus here is on the air component of the conference, it is reasonable to speculate on what may have terminated the war earlier, had room been made for negotiations with Germany. Instead, the air war would go on with destruction and death reaching unimaginable proportions.

It was Air Marshall Portal who advocated strategic area bombing of German industrial facilities. Arthur Harris led RAF Bomber Command under Portal's direction. Their relationship would prove tenuous at best.

Happy Valley

A prime example of the RAF war effort was undertaken in the Ruhr Valley, known to both RAF and U.S. Eighth Air Force crews as "Happy Valley," and the core of German industrial might. Targeted cities were heavily defended by Germany's own integrated system consisting of search radars, flak batteries, searchlights and night fighters equipped with airborne radar – a defensive network that would come at a high price for the attacking strike forces. The RAF opened the campaign on 10 March 1943 with an attack on Essen, brought in with the Pathfinder Force. Essen was attacked again on the night of 12 March, then Duisburg on the 26 March. RAF operations in the Ruhr continued until mid-July. Essen and Duisburg were hit again in April, and in May Dortmund, Dusseldorf (I went there in a B-17 on September 9, 1944) and Wuppertal were also hit. There were 43 attacks on Ruhr cities by July's end, at a cost of 5,000 aircrew and an estimated 15,000 German civilians.

At this point, Harris, with Churchill's positive input, decided to go after Hamburg with the objective of destroying Germany's prime port and second largest city. Hamburg was also the first of Combined RAF/Eighth Air Force Operations – Round the Clock Bombing.

Hamburg

Hamburg illustrates a prime example of combined RAF and

Eighth Air Force operations, carrying forward the Round the Clock Bombing concept introduced by Ira Eaker at Casablanca. The combined attacks on Hamburg in the week 24 July through 2 August 1943 were called "Blitz Week." The effort is summarized in the table below.

Hamburg Objectives: Factories, Submarine Base, Oil Refineries		
Date	Attacking Force	Aircraft Deployed
24 July 1943	RAF Night Area Bombing	791
25 July 1943	Eighth AF Daylight Strike	100
26 July 1943	Eighth AF Daylight Strike	54
26 July 1943	RAF Night, Set Off Alarms	6
27 July 1943	RAF Night Area Bombing	729
29 July 1943	RAF Night Area Bombing	777
2 August 1943	RAF Night Area Bombing	318

German Air defenses at Hamburg consisted of:

- Area search radars

- Night fighters with airborne radar – Bf-110s, Ju 88s

- Day fighters – Bf 109s, Fw 190s

- 278 88mm flak guns

- 24 searchlight batteries

The devastating results:

- 87 RAF Aircraft lost

- 17 Eighth Air Force Aircraft lost

- 552 British and American men killed

- Hamburg: 60 percent of the city was destroyed, including factories, schools, churches, shops, and homes

- Hamburg: More than 42,000 civilians died in the firestorm

It is stupefying to ponder the plight of civilians subjected to seven days and nights of fire bombing, their agonies in dying, and the utter destruction of their city. I call Hiroshima the second coming of Hamburg.

The Dam Busters

Perhaps the most illustrative real life story of British technological ingenuity is that of the dam busters – the stuff of which populates movie scripts with all the components of suspense and action that one might expect in a film thriller. In fact, there was a film made with that title in 1954. Taking out German dams was already on the radar screen of RAF strategists as an option of flooding the Ruhr Valley. An eccentric 55 year old British scientist named Barnes Wallis designed a bouncing bomb – he called it a "spherical bomb" – capable of hitting naval ships (bouncing over protective nets) and breaching dams if delivered to a vulnerable point on the dam's structure. He approached Avro designer Roy Chadwick to assess design parameters and the possibilities of an aircraft capable of handling outsize bombs. What fell out of this was "Upkeep," a bomb in the shape of a 55 gallon drum. When released at a low altitude and appropriate air speed the bomb would skip along the surface of the reservoir to hit and rupture the dam wall, resulting in flooding of areas of the Ruhr facing the dam, depriving industrial facilities of electricity and its people of water. The initial reaction from Harris when briefed on the proposal was negative, but when Wallis showed Harris a film of a prototype bomb being dropped, he won support and Harris gave the order to form a special squadron to undertake the mission, suggesting also that RAF Wing Commander Guy Gibson command it. Winston Churchill also favored the idea and gave the go ahead for testing.

The bomb was suspended in an exposed position under the Lancaster's bomb bay. The top and bottom of the drum-like structure pointed to the wing tips. Thus, when released and contacting the reservoir's surface, the bomb would pick up the force to induce the necessary rotation to make it skip on its way to the dam's wall. The rotation would pull the bomb toward the base of the wall's structure where it would explode. Wallis had worked out the aircraft delivery parameters that required a precise aircraft speed of 240 mph and release altitude of 60 feet. Altitude control by the pilot was demanding. Two light beacons would be mounted fore and aft on the belly of the aircraft. Pilot altitude control inputs found 60 feet when the two beams' footprints met on the surface, indicating that the aircraft was precisely 60 feet above the water's surface. These requirements made their way into the extensive training program undertaken to get the aircrews ready for the mission.

As Harris suggested, Guy Gibson, an experienced Lancaster and night fighter pilot, was chosen to lead the effort. Gibson in turn chose his pilots with great care. Delivery techniques were so complicated that intensive training would have to be undertaken to master them. These crews included RAF personnel of several different nationalities, as well as members of the Royal Australian Air Force (RAAF), Royal Canadian Air Force (RCAF) and Royal New Zealand Air Force (RNZAF).

Three dams with flood plains facing the Ruhr Valley were

identified as the prime targets; the Mohne, Sorpe and Eder. *Operation Chastise* attacks would be at night with maximum moonlight and were scheduled for the night of 16/17 May 1943. The operation was assigned to RAF No. 5 Group, the new squadron formed for the mission, initially called Squadron "X," as the speed of its formation outstripped the RAF process for naming squadrons. Formed in secrecy, it would become Squadron 617.

Three Lancaster "waves" were set up for the attacks. The first, Formation 1, consisted of nine aircraft led by Guy Gibson. The Mohne dam was the designated target. Formation 1 took off in elements of three aircraft separated by 10 minutes.

The Lancasters flew at low altitudes – as low as 100 feet – to stay under detection by German search radars as they penetrated enemy territory. Just try that some night for thrills, even with moonlight. One of the en route Lancasters crashed after hitting high power electric lines.

Formation 2 consisted of five aircraft led by Flight Lieutenant Joe McCarthy, an American volunteer from New York City. McCarthy's group actually took off first, since they had the longer route to the target area. The assigned target was the Sorpe dam, and en route to the target area the force took a beating. Two had to return – one due to damage from ground fire, and a second was damaged when it hit the surface while taking evasive action. Two more were assaulted by ground fire over the Netherlands – both crashed and burned taking the lives of fourteen crew members. Formation 3, led by Pilot Officer Warner Ottley, was a reserve of five Lancasters to take off two hours after the others and attack any of the dams left standing.

With his formation now over Mohne, Gibson swept in on the first run under intense fire and released his "Upkeep" that performed as designed. It skipped into Mohne's concrete wall and exploded under water. It was a perfect hit, but the wall was not breached. Gibson made a second run at the target to draw flak away from succeeding runs by wingmen Flight Lieutenants John Hopgood, Harold Martin, David Maltby, and Squadron Leader Henry Young. Hopgood made the next run under increasingly intense ground fire. With a wing segment already burning, his bomb was released, but it bounced over the dam and exploded beyond. Hopgood's Lancaster crashed; his crew made it out, but he did not. Successive runs by Martin, Young and Maltby, were successful, and Mohne's concrete wall was breached. A wall of water twenty feet high poured into the breach, rolling on in a wave toward the Ruhr Valley.

After the Mohne action, Gibson led the Lancasters that had not dropped their Upkkeeps to the Eder. The approach to the Eder was difficult because of the hilly topography, but it was undefended. The Eder dam was attacked by four of the Lancasters, two of which scored hits with their Upkeeps – one by Flight Lieutenant Dave Shannon with no effect, but the second, flown by Pilot Officer Leslie Knight, caused a large breach. On a third run by Squadron Leader Henry Maudslay, the bomb hit the structure and exploded, but Maudslay's Lancaster was damaged by the blast. His aircraft was shot down en route to his base in England. Ironically, the Eder dam had nothing to do with the water supply to the Ruhr.

The Sorpe structure was much different from those of the Eder or Mohne – its wall was a huge earthen mound and the most unlikely to be breached. Flight Lieutenant Joe McCarthy made nine runs before his bombardier was satisfied, and the Upkeep was dropped on the tenth. It hit and exploded, but only a section of the crest was blown away. Sorpe remained intact.

The strikes were only partially successful in terms of military expectations. Flooding was extensive as reported by the pilot of a reconnaissance aircraft the morning following the attacks. There was, however, no significant effect on Ruhr industry. By 27 June water output was restored and the electrical grid was at full power output. German architect Albert Speer, Minister of Arms and War Production, launched a massive manpower effort to restore the breaches. Scaffolding had to be erected facing the breaches for Speer's labor force. His great fear was a repeat by the RAF while this work was ongoing, but there would be no re-strike.

The cost was unusually high for aircrews. Of the 133 crew members who participated 53 were killed – that's more than a third. Of the 19 Lancasters dispatched, eight did not return. German casualties are estimated at 1,600.

Earthquake Bombs

The Barnes Wallis story does not end with Upkeeps, as he returned to his earlier quest for a super bomb. Among Wallis' unique designs for selective destruction were "Tallboy" and "Grand Slam," thought of as "earthquake" bombs, for good reason. They penetrated deeply and moved the earth at the base of the structure intended. Tallboy was a monstrous 12,000 pounds in destructive power weighing in at 10,000 pounds. It was effective against hardened structures and used against submarine pens and for *Operation Crossbow* that went after V-1 flying bomb sites. It was a Tallboy aboard a Lancaster that sank the battleship Tirpitz in November 1944.

Grand Slam was a king size gorilla – 22,000 pounds of destruction. Grand Slam could penetrate even more deeply, with the goal of shifting the ground at the impact point. It was also effective against hardened buildings and used extensively to attack hardened U-Boat havens. It is worth noting that the Lancaster had the capability to handle an outsize payload of Grand Slam proportions. Both bombs were used in the latter stages of the air campaign.

The Battle Of Berlin, Related Operations

On 19 August 1943, in a letter to the Air Ministry citing the apparent successes of raids on Regensburg and Hamburg, Winston Churchill suggested to Charles Portal such attacks be extended to Berlin. When conveyed to Arthur Harris, it was all he needed. Harris had held that Berlin was the key to victory, and he wrote to Churchill indicating that planning would proceed accordingly. Still a major bone of contention, however, was the issue of targeting priorities. Focusing on Berlin would depart from Allied policy directives to bomb aircraft and ball bearing production. Portal found himself between the proverbial rock and a hard spot; he favored the adopted allied strategy, but at the same time was reluctant to override Harris' intention to proceed with destroying Berlin. Harris established rapport directly with Churchill in his frequent visits to Chequers Court – the latter's wartime residence. There was much correspondence on the issue between Portal and Harris, in which Portal displayed great patience in expressing his position. Harris' replies were negative, as he alluded to unclear tactical reasons in why he could not conform to the directives. He remained committed to a Berlin mission with the same objectives used on Regensburg and Hamburg. Weekly visits to Chequers worked as a sanctuary for Harris during the dispute on Berlin, but the issue of the Allied directive would surface again.

The Battle of Berlin, begun by the RAF in November 1943, shares some characteristics with the Battle of Britain. Both spanned a matter of months, both were costly in terms of aircraft and airmen lost and both countries failed to achieve intended results. Arthur Harris had convinced the Air Staff that he could deliver the fatal blow, "It will cost us between 400 and 500 aircraft. It will cost Germany the war." Harris had the aircraft and aircrew resources to deploy as many as 800 bombers on any mission. One might relate that thinking to the week-long attacks on Hamburg and the still ongoing fire bombing strategy to destroy German industries and beat populations into submission. The Berlin plan went forward in the winter months from 18 November 1943 and ran through 31 March 1944. There were 18 attacks on Berlin and other German cities during that period, generally regarded as "The Battle Of Berlin." Winter months were essential. Darkness was an RAF requisite for bombing, and the months planned for this effort would yield maximum darkness for the long trek to Berlin and back.

A lead effort against Berlin, that would define the combat environment over Germany, was flown on 23 August 1943. Some 600 RAF aircraft led by Pathfinders penetrated the *Kammuber Line*, Germany's first line of defense against air attacks. With a loss of two aircraft as they flew on to Berlin, they knew an integrated and deadly system of defense awaited them. The incoming bomber stream faced both day and radar-equipped night fighters, intense flak and searchlights capable of "coning" British bombers for easy pickings. A new Luftwaffe defensive tactic was introduced with the radar-equipped Bf 110, also manned with four guns firing at an upward angle. Called *Wilde Sau* (Wild Boar) and guided by radar, these BF 110s would slip under the belly of the RAF bomber and fire their upward pointing guns into the victim. The tactic was tested over Peenemunde on 17 August with positive results. Forty RAF bombers were shot down that night. The new technique would prove deadly for the RAF.

Harris' order of battle included attacks by the Lancaster, Halifax, Mosquito and the Sterling on Berlin and other German cities. The Lancaster was the dominant aircraft. The Sterling was taken out of the battle early due to perceived vulnerability.

The counterpoint to the RAF campaign was Herman Goering's plan to make London suffer equally with what was called "the baby blitz," to be launched by the Luftwaffe also in the winter months.

Using their twin-engine aircraft (they had no long- range four engine bombers) – Ju 88s, Ju 188s, Do 217s, Me 410s and the He 177 – they attacked London en masse on 21 January 1944. The raid was a complete failure – only 32 out of 282 bombs dropped hit the capital. Attacks continued for the next four months from the Luftwaffe's French airfields. Results were limited, and of the 515 aircraft gathered for the effort, 329 were lost. It was almost as though the Luftwaffe had no operational memory of the original Blitz.

Berlin was hit again the night of 31 August – 1 September with another 333 aircrew fed into the conflagration. Another 16 bombers and 130 aircrew were lost over Munich 3 – 4 September. At this point Harris decided on a pause in bombing operations to give the RAF more time to resolve the Wilde Sau problem.

On 22 October, an RAF force of over 500 bombers attacked the city of Kassel. Incendiaries ignited firestorms that brought death and destruction on a scale paralleling that of Hamburg. Harris now claimed that 19 German cities had been reduced to "virtual" destruction by the bombing campaign, and identified 60 additional cities on his list of those to be dealt with. After that, mop up operations were all that was left on the agenda of victory. Harris invited the Americans to join the effort, but that would not happen, as the USAAF opted to stay with the goals established by the adoption of POINTBLANK at the Casablanca Conference.

In summary, starting with 18 November 1943, regarded by historians as the start of the Battle of Berlin, through 2 January 1944, there were 11 major operations by RAF Bomber Command. Ten of these struck Berlin with a force size averaging 495 aircraft. One of the 11 attacks flew against Leipzig with a force of 527 bombers.

Starting on 21 January 1943, there were 17 raids against German cities; six of these were against Berlin, the eleven remaining were against other major German cities. Harris' strategy was to include other cities in order to disburse Luftwaffe defenses. British losses were appalling. The Nuremburg mission was a disaster for the RAF. Berlin and Nuremburg held great symbolism for Harris – Berlin was Hitler's capitol city, and Nuremburg, more importantly, was the birthplace of the Nazi party. Harris sent 795 aircraft on the attack. The cost was 96 aircraft, a staggering 20.6 percent. Damage to Nuremburg was minimal, 265 buildings of no military importance were hit, 75 people were killed and 11,000 were made homeless.

The effort cost Bomber Command dearly: 2,690 airmen killed with another 1,000 as prisoners of war. Overall for the Battle of Berlin, a total of 499 aircraft of all types were lost at an unacceptable attrition rate of 4.9 percent. It is estimated that civilian deaths were 7,480 with 2,194 missing. Injuries were 17, 092 and 817,730 made homeless. One can only imagine the extent of destruction.

On 3 February 1944, Eighth Bomber Command launched one of its 1,000 airplane raids on the city of Berlin under the guise of THUNDERCLAP, a plan devised earlier as the best way to pave the way for the advance of the Russian army. Aiming points in the city ran the gamut: Unter den Linden boulevard, Brandenburg Gate, the Friederichstrasse Station and the Reichstag building that housed the German Imperial Diet, or parliament. Friederichstrasse Station was littered with people fleeing the Russian advance. Hap Arnold signed on to the plan for an attack on Berlin calling for something dramatic and brutal. George Marshall also signed on, calling for heavy and relentless attacks from the air. When Lt Gen Carl Spaatz presented his "Oil Plan" for bombing to Jimmy Doolittle on 30 January, Doolittle objected, calling the plan immoral and pointless terror bombing. Doolittle had no sympathy from Spaatz for his views, nor had he much choice. The mission went forward, and thousands died. The mission, at best, marks the point of America's entry into the business of area bombing, and the drift of our commitment to focus on precision attacks against strategic targets.

It is fair to pose the question as to where one comes down on success or failure during war. Given the intent as articulated by Harris – 500 bombers against German cities will end the war – the rational was to destroy industries and their labor force in those cities and to terrorize inhabitants. But results were minimal in regard to ending the war. The cost in terms of human life was almost beyond comprehension, to say nothing of loss of aircraft and the destruction of property in all its forms. Given the intent, it would be hard to agree with any of Harris' conclusions on the central issue. Some think otherwise, especially those airmen that flew for Harris and hold another perspective. Sir Michael Beetham – 10 operations to Berlin – disagrees that the Battle of Berlin was a failure. He suggests in his book, *The Hardest Victory*, that the outcome would have been different if Harris had more aircraft (as he had demanded) and more time to continue. Others argue that the RAF bombing campaign progressively weakened Germany and hastened the war's end. One thing seems certain to me, the Battle of Berlin was overtaken by Operation Overlord – the Battle of Normandy. But that hardly stopped the bombing, as we will see.

Dresden

By February 1945, the city of Dresden was filled with German refugees escaping the onset of the Russian Army. On 13 February, 244 RAF Lancasters attacked the city of Dresden, an architectural and cultural gem among German cities, comparable in size to Manchester. The next night a second wave of RAF bombers attacked Chemnitz, near Dresden. On 15 February the Eighth Bomber Command attacked Dresden's marshaling yards. Dresden lay in ruins after these attacks and has emerged as a model for challenging the rational for area bombing. Dresden became a wasteland with firestorms equal to those of Hamburg, consuming the city and its inhabitants. The Eighth Air Force attacked Dresden one more time before the war ended.

Arguments about the validity of attacks on Dresden have persisted for years. There was no true strategic objective in terms of war industry in Dresden. One reason put forward was that Dresden had become a haven for fleeing German troops, and the justification for the attacks lay in denying the German army the opportunity to regroup. Another reason was that Dresden was a key transportation center. According to the historian Roger Freeman, the Russians called for the Dresden strike for this reason. At this stage the German war effort was barely alive, and all Germany lay in ruins. The retrospective indictment holds that the Dresden attacks were nothing more than punishment. Similar debates concerning Hiroshima have evolved as we Americans noted in 1995, the 50th anniversary of both events. Were they necessary? I have always felt that the Dresden affair was akin to a knee jerk reaction in the process of selecting targets. The power was there – simply looking for some place to be applied. For Great Britain, however, this was not an issue. Yet, with Dresden, the moral imperative began to resonate and does to this day with bombing then (and now) in its many new dimensions.

RAF raids continued under Arthur Harris's direction: Dessau on 7 – 8 March, Essen on 11 March, 12 March on Dortmund and 16 March Wurzburg yet again. By 9:20 PM, Wurzburg was engulfed in flames, and the architectural history spanning centuries was utterly destroyed. From 1 – 27 March the RAF bombed 13 German cities. The Eighth went after oil, transportation and factories while the 15th Air Force attacked transportation and oil targets from bases in Italy. March 1945 is considered the peak of bombing operations by the combined air campaign against Germany.

In a letter to General Hastings Ismay on March 28, Winston Churchill expressed concern to his chief military assistant over the process of bombing German cities to wreak terror. He called for more precise concentration on military objectives such as oil and communications. Churchill later called for a review of the effectiveness of area bombing from the standpoint of British interests. The seeds of doubt were now planted, though not yet flowering.

In the end, from September 1939 to September 1945, 55,573 young men of RAF Bomber Command would die. RAF Fighter Command lost 3,690 killed during the same period. The Eighth Bomber Command total deaths were 26,000, but these casualties were incurred over a much shorter period of time, 1942 until the war in Europe ended in May 1945. Civilian deaths from the bombing of German cities are estimated at 600,000. 36 This does not cover the numbers of German airmen who would die. The cost in human life is simply staggering.

Arthur Harris was made Marshal of the RAF in 1946 and retired in September of that year. The rising tide of resentment flagged by the bombing of Dresden followed Harris like a hound dog into his retirement years. He refused a peerage when Bomber Command's aircrews were denied a campaign medal, essentially snubbed by those belatedly finding their consciences. In 1953, Churchill, once again Prime Minister, offered Harris a baronetcy, which he accepted. His aircrews came together as a veterans' organization to defend their commander. In 1992 his statue was unveiled at the RAF Chapel St. Clement Danes by Queen Elizabeth, but the event was marred by jeering protesters. Despite all this, the veterans who flew under his leadership still revere him. By now known as "Bomber" or "Butcher," Harris died in 1984 at age 91. Regarding Dresden, he acknowledged the destruction of a beautiful city, but "Here I will only say that the attack on Dresden was at the time considered a military necessity by much more important people than myself."

My own view is that the image of Harris is that of the Jamaican voodoo doll in which pins of venom are stuck by vindictive ill wishers. The architecture of area bombing rose from the prophets of doom, supported by the Air Staff and approved by Churchill, Roosevelt and the politics of the time; leaders who could hide from the moral issues in the heat of war. Harris carried it forward for them.

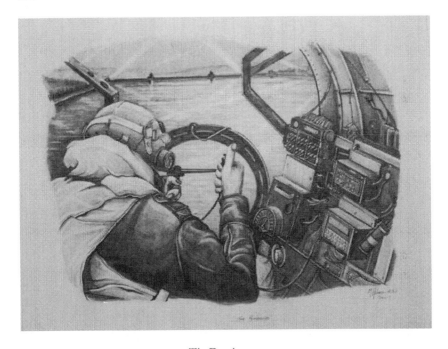

The Dambusters

69

Down in the Drink

Sighting the Towers

Harry's Office

Shot Down and on the Run

CHAPTER 5 AMERICA AWAKENS

America in the 1930s was beset with complex cultural, racial, and ethnic divisions. The economic excesses and social indulgences of the 1920s led to the destruction of the economy by 1930, ushering in the crippling depression that paralyzed the nation for a decade. Jobs evaporated as production ground to a halt. Morale collapsed and crushing poverty became rampant, as a helpless government could only observe the nation's, as well as the world's, descent into the morass.

Many of the programs developed by President Roosevelt in the early 1930s gave people new hope as the nation struggled to recover. By 1939, recovery began in earnest, but it was built primarily upon the bloody, gossamer base of munitions production, to eventually feed the conflict erupting in Europe.

During the 1930s the forty-eight states were united constitutionally and geographically, but ironically in name only. In its idyllic self-image, the U.S. was the great melting pot in which the American promise would somehow blend its diverse elements into a homogeneous national culture. In reality, however, America was a nation of deep divisions and conflicting interests. Residual hatreds from the Civil War haunted us; the North and South still maintained their differences in religions, speech patterns, and customs that kept them separate entities within the contiguous national boundary that was loosely the Union. Racism was alive and flourishing both in the South and North. Religious demagogues fanned the fires of hatred with their political harangues and diatribes in the name of Christianity. Ethnic divisions set people apart in hostile camps with almost the same intensity as race, and as Europe drifted toward war, ethnic sentiments tended to polarize within European counterparts. At the same time, a grassroots isolationist movement vigorously opposed any involvement whatsoever in foreign wars.

The German Nazi movement rubbed off on their American ethnic counterparts in the form of a splinter group known as the German-American Bund. In New York before the war, I watched them parade pompously in their brown shirts and swastikas preaching their message of Aryan supremacy. There were also the Mussolini fascists, communists and socialists. New dimensions in criminal activity were ushered in as the result of prohibition, regarded in retrospect as the "noble experiment." If there was any unifying force at work in this ethnic olio, it was the English language. The population mix today, with Asian and Hispanic groups now among the leading players, in many ways mirrors that of the 1930s. That mirror image begins to focus further when considering today's splinter groups of neo-fascists and self-proclaimed "minutemen" at war with our government and the new dimensions of violence they have brought to the American scene.

All of the divisions that defined America in the 1930s were swept aside by Pearl Harbor, perhaps the greatest miscalculation in modern times. Heterogeneous America did not disappear, but its divisions would lie festering out of sight for some time to come, as the country found a unifying cause. I was swept along in the tides of that time and absorbed by the explosion of American air power.

Hitler's aggressions in the mid-1930s rose to our consciousness with the invasion of Poland in 1939, the beginning of six years of total warfare in what would be the most consuming and widespread war in the history of the world. One must bear in mind that the United States military at this time was woefully unprepared in all of its naval, land, and air components, as compared with the German and Japanese war machines. The navy was perhaps best prepared in terms of readiness with 15 battleships, 5 aircraft carriers, 38 cruisers, and over 200 destroyers, most of the latter dating back to WW I. Our regular Army consisted of 130,000 enlisted men and officers, with a National Guard of 175,000 and a reserve officers' corps of 70,000. Our Army Air Force was pitifully weak with a 1,700 tactical and training aircraft and 20,000 enlisted men and officers. It was on this foundation that mobilization of the nation would evolve in the coming war years. Bear in mind that in 1939 there was still no strong mood for mobilization, with "no more wars in Europe" a dominant frame of mind among the public, and the basic tenet of the isolationist movement.

Strategy

Blueprints for the U.S. strategic bombing campaign began to take root before Pearl Harbor, as President Roosevelt reacted to the fall of Western Europe and concerned himself with the survival of Great Britain. Roosevelt was greatly influenced by Winston Churchill and his own conviction that the futures of both countries were linked by common political and cultural ties. Roosevelt had already anticipated our direct involvement in the war. Indeed, some say he promoted it. While, as I have noted, there was certainly no common public consensus for intervention on our part at the time, as Hitler triumphed in 1940 and 1941, American public opinion did begin to swing in favor of some active support for Great Britain, short of full intervention. The Battle of Britain was a factor.

Early in 1941, Roosevelt requested the U.S. Army's War Plans Division to consider contingency planning in the event of our direct involvement. Thus military planners began to articulate strategic applications of American air power. Assuming Germany and Japan as the enemy, U.S. Army War Plans Division developed the initial strategic plan for the application of air power:

U.S. Air Power Strategy in 1941, Pre-Pearl Harbor
• Defend the Western Hemisphere
• Prosecute a sustained air offensive against Germany
• Support strategic defense in the Pacific
• Provide air support for the invasion of Europe
• Continue strategic air operations against Germany until its collapse
• Concentrate maximum strategic air power to support the defeat of Japan

War planners viewed the primary goal as the defeat of Germany by disrupting her electrical power, transportation, petroleum, and manufacturing systems.

With the attack on Pearl Harbor on 7 December 1941 and Germany's declaration of war on 11 December, all the barriers of public perceptions and factional political divisions evaporated. Later that month, at the ARCADIA Conference, the U.S. and Great Britain declared the total defeat of Germany as their top priority. The grand strategy was to apply all military might to that objective. At the Casablanca Conference in January of 1943, Allied air planners became much more definitive in laying down the basic strategy for the air campaign.

As noted in Chapter 4, the Casablanca Conference defined strategic bombing objectives and the Combined Bomber Operations (CBO) strategy leading to the "round the clock" bombing offensive by the USAAF and the RAF. The CBO's objective set forth in operation POINTBLANK was to destroy or neutralize 60 key targets essential to Germany's war effort. Top priority was given to the destruction of German fighter aircraft capability in the realization of air superiority. POINTBLANK's target list included aircraft manufacturing, ball bearings, petroleum, steel, electrical power, machine tools, transportation systems, rubber, armament production, and other key manufacturing elements in German war production. The plan was based on an invasion of occupied France in the spring of 1944. The USAAF structure required in 1943 to implement this plan was phased as follows:

USAAF 1943 Force Structure Plan	
Aircraft, by Date	**Penetration Depth**
800 heavy bombers by July 1943	Limited to range of escort fighters
1,192 heavy bombers by October 1943	400 miles
1,746 heavy bombers by January 1944	500 miles
2,702 heavy bombers by March 1944	Limited only by aircraft radius of action

It is interesting to note that the U.S. delivery of aircraft and air crews as they were fed into the Eighth Air Force kept pace with the plan, something that I regard in retrospect as a miracle in production, logistics and training. My 487th Bomb Group was among those organized in 1943 to meet the expansion required by the plan. The time span from the inception of the plan at the Casablanca Conference to its force structure high point in March of 1944 was barely over two years.

Military aviation technology in the 1930s was evolving rapidly with arming nations following different paths. Germany, Japan, and

Russia were all driving technology toward tactical uses of air power. Germany, for example, developed the Junkers Ju 87 Stuka dive bomber as a tactical weapon and used it effectively in its invasion of Poland in 1939.

Level bombing techniques developed by Germany concentrated on twin-engine platforms such as the Dornier Do 17, Junkers Ju 88 and Heinkel He 111. These medium-range aircraft were effective in the operational environment in which they performed, especially in the attacks on London during the Blitz. Germany did develop the four-engine Fw 200 C3 bomber and had it operational in 1940. The aircraft had a range of 2,200 miles and was about the size of a B-17, but it was used for maritime patrols in the North and Baltic Seas and for attacks on naval and merchant ships. Later German experiments produced several four-engine, long-range prototypes like the He 274 (range 2,640 miles), He 277 (range 4,475 miles), and the Me 264. The latter had a range of over 9,300 miles and was designed to reach New York. The prototype Me 264 flew in December, 1942. None of these aircraft reached production as Germany focused its aircraft industry on fighters. The evolving V-2 missile may well have conditioned German strategy with regard to long-range bombing platforms. Russia never developed a long-range capability, focusing its aircraft development on air defense and tactical support for ground forces. As we have seen in Great Britain's air staff belief that "the bomber would always get through," the spotlight was on bomber development during the 1930s, but there was equal concern with air defense. Aircraft development efforts produced both fighters and bombers.

The B-17

The U.S. followed the path toward strategic, long-range, heavy bombers, and by 1935 the concept emerged as a reality when Boeing produced its Model 299, the prototype of the B-17, which would evolve as America's premier bombing platform in the European campaign. However, none of the aircraft delivery systems available in the early 1930s, including Boeing's Model 299, had the capability of achieving effective bombing in terms of accuracy, payload, or range.

The YB version of the B-17 was delivered in 1937 and with it the Army Air Corp's first modern bomber, which could match contemporary Air Corps fighter speeds, yet fly higher, and also achieve long range. With such performance characteristics and its armament for self-protection, the B-17 theoretically could take care of itself in any circumstance.

Defensive armament for the B-17A – D models would prove, however, to be woefully inadequate for reasons associated with those notions about high speed performance. These early models had no power turrets or tail guns. There were two manually operated "flexible" guns in the waist, a flexible dorsal gun on top, and a ventral gun or "bath tub" slung under the fuselage, also manually operated. This too, would all change with the advent of the actual battle scene. As defensive fire power evolved, the army decided to make use of the .50 caliber machine gun. Power turrets and tail guns were introduced with the B-17E model, and by the time the B-17G reached production, there were power turrets in the nose, top fuselage, ball turret below, and twin 50s manually operated in the tail position. These powered turrets and tail position twin 50s were complemented by hand-operated flexible guns in the waist, nose, and radio operator's compartment.

The Norden Bombsight

When Hitler invaded Poland in 1939, the U. S. Army Air Corps had only 23 B-17 aircraft in its bomber force. Others, such as the B-18, were already obsolete; and the B-24 was still on the drawing boards. The evolution of the B-17 as a strategic bomber was complemented by the development of the Norden bombsight, which proved to yield remarkable precision and accuracy by the standards of the time, from altitudes of 20,000 feet. Along with the adoption of the .50 caliber machine gun, the Norden bombsight was one of the technological drivers that brought the American daylight bombing concept to reality. This bombsight, originally designed for the Navy by C. L. Norden, was under development since 1932. Test drops from high altitude into the dry lake range at Muroc, California in ideal weather conditions led to claims by our Army fliers of the late 1930s that they could put a bomb in a pickle barrel from 20,000 feet. The real world of daylight strategic bombing, however, would prove otherwise. The Norden sight was extremely accurate in the hands of a skilled bombardier, but results depended on good visibility, tight formation, and a smoothly flown bomb run.

Superchargers

The development of turbo superchargers for aircraft engines was another key technological factor in the B-17's performance. Superchargers were essential to compensate for greatly reduced air densities as altitude increased by maintaining surface-level atmospheric density in engine carburetors, as the aircraft climbed to and maintained high altitude. In turn, the high altitude reached produced true airspeeds in excess of 300 miles per hour. The B-17's airspeed at such altitudes exceeded that of contemporary American fighters in the 1930s. In the minds of American strategists, this was the main ingredient for defense against enemy fighters – they could be outrun. This, too, would prove not to be the case.

The B-24

A prototype version of the B-24 took to the air in 1939. Theoretical performance of the B-24 was based on its high aspect ratio wing design. In theory the B-24 had greater range and payload than the B-17. While this edge existed at medium altitudes – say 10,000 feet – its performance at high altitude would be disappointing. That high aspect ratio wing gave a much smaller aerodynamic surface than that of the B-17, making the B-24 more dependent upon the denser air of lower altitudes. It was a bitch to hold in formation at 20,000 feet, believe me.

The Fw 190

The Focke-Wulf 190 *Würger* (Shrike) grew from roots in 1937, when the German Ministry of Aviation called for design proposals from aircraft manufacturers for a new fighter aircraft to take its place alongside the renowned Bf 109. In a sense, the new fighter would be an upgraded aircraft capable of competing with new foreign designs under development. Among a range of proposed power options under consideration, Designer Kurt Tank caught the eye of the Aviation Ministry with a proposal for an aircraft equipped with the 14 cylinder air cooled radial – the BMW 139. Aircraft with radial engines at the time were considered to have limited performance due to excessive drag in the engine's large frontal area housed under a cowling. Tank thought otherwise on witnessing the performance of U.S. Navy aircraft equipped with radials, and had the view that upgraded streamlining could mitigate the drag effects of radials by "shaping" the flow of air as it entered the cowling to increase the total air flow around the engine, thereby reducing the size of the opening. The Aviation Ministry favored the idea because of hot competition for in line engines used by many Luftwaffe aircraft.

Tank's design also featured a wide track inward retracting landing gear giving it much better ground handling techniques and far fewer landing and take off accidents than the Bf 109, that suffered greatly because of its narrow track gear that folded inward. The design also featured other new ideas such as a bubble canopy over the cockpit area greatly increasing pilot visibility.

Both nimble and powerful, the Fw 190 would make its mark as both an interceptor and fighter bomber. The Fw 190 appeared over France in the summer of 1941 and its first use in combat on the Eastern Front added a significant dimension to the Luftwaffe's capability. However, as an interceptor, its altitude capability was marginalized above 20,000 feet. The 190's BMW 801 engine lacked a two stage supercharger needed to reach altitudes above 20,000 feet, and had a short wing that did not generate enough lift at higher altitudes. Modifications to the aircraft would eventually resolve the altitude limitations. The D series of the aircraft introduced *Langnasen Dora* – or the long nose Fw 190 as we know it. The BMW 801 engine was replaced with the Jumo 213A, 12 cylinder in-line inverted "V." Assembly of the Doras began in August 1944 with a total of 1,805 produced. Ironically, having resolved the altitude problem, the Fw 190D saw little use against USAAF bombers and was directed to ground support which had priority at this stage of the war.

The prototype Fw 190 (V1) first flew on 1 June 1939 showing good performance for a small aircraft – with excellent handling qualities. A later prototype, the V5, was equipped with the upgraded BMW 801 C-0 engine rated at 1,539 hp. The V5 made its first flight in the spring of 1940. Later pre-production models were armed with two synchronized 7.92 mm MG 17 machine guns located in the forward fuselage and one MG 17 in each wing firing outside the arc of the propeller.

Starting with the A series, modification steps to the aircraft ranged numerically from A-0 to A-9 with engine upgrades, armament package variations and structural changes to the air frame through each series step.

Testing the prototypes continued until the aircraft went into production. Some 50 modifications were made before it was certified by the Aviation Ministry for deployment to operational units. The first of the A-1 series with its BMW 801 C-1 engine rated at 1,539 hp was delivered in June 1941 and entered active service with JG 26 stationed in the Paris area. Armament was two wing root MG 17s and two fuselage mounted MG 17s – all four were synchronized to fire through the propeller arc – plus two 20 mm cannons, one in each wing.

Series A-2 through A-5 went forward with continuing upgrades for improved performance. With the advent of the V-5 series, the Fw 190 would be waiting for the Eighth Bomber Command. Over 1700 V-5s were produced by June 1943. A-6 modifications were made to address shortcoming in dealing with U.S. B-17s and B-24s. Armament was upgraded to include two MG 17 fuselage guns and four 20 mm cannons – two in the wing root and two in the outer sections of the wing with expanded ammunition boxes.

The A-8 version of the aircraft went into production in February 1944 in both armor, armament and engine performance. It was the A-8 aircraft that evolved as the *Sturmbock* (Battering Ram), used tactically by the *Sturmgruppen* – the storm troopers of the Luftwaffe – in attacks en masse against Eighth Bomber Command formations. Protective armor was installed around the cockpit and other critical components. The outer wing 20 mm cannons were replaced with 30 mm MK 108 cannons, a formidable array of fire power – four cannons in the wing and two fuselage mounted machine guns. Over 6,500 Fw 190 A-8s were produced.

The tally of Fw 190 A series production during WW II exceeded 13,000.

Sunrise Over Lavenham

CHAPTER 6   EIGHTH AIR FORCE

Pearl Harbor had the effect, among many other catastrophes, of hastening mobilization already begun to new imperatives. None of this accelerated pressure was lost on General Henry "Hap" Arnold and his staff. A graduate of West Point Military Academy, Arnold was one of the originals; trained by the Wright Brothers, he was one of the first three rated pilots in the Air Force and a protégé and disciple of Billy Mitchell. Arnold was a key factor in the development and expansion of the U.S. Army Air Service in WW I and the Army Air Corps on the eve of WW II. In 1942, he became Commanding General of the U.S. Army Air Force, a position he would hold throughout WW II and beyond, with the final rank of a five star general.

Hap Arnold held sway over the creation and buildup of the U.S. Army Air Force. Early in 1942, the deployment of combat components in the form of numbered air forces (e.g., The Eighth Air Force) worldwide was already in progress. Recognition of the sweeping dimensions of the war in Europe led to the creation of an airborne armada capable of taking the air force's plans for strategic bombing from concept to practical execution. The Eighth Air Force would be that armada. It began its active life on 2 January 1942 in Savannah, Georgia, where in fact its historical roots remain and are still recognized by people of that fair city. General Ira C. Eaker was named to lead the newly created Eighth Air Force. Although he had no combat experience in the WW I, Eaker flew fighters in the interim between the wars and was a firm proponent of the U.S. Army Air Force's concept of applying strategic bombing to a war winning outcome. Eaker knew he would be working alongside the RAF and its night operations with a force operating in daylight. Also critical to his needs, he knew that achieving an operational capability in the European wartime environment and direct support from the RAF was essential.

Two months after Pearl Harbor, Eaker, now commanding the Eighth, was sent to England with a small staff to lay the framework for the American bombing campaign against Hitler's occupied Europe. Eaker arrived on 20 February 1942 with a small staff of six officers in tow, including Lt Col Frank Armstrong, who would become one of the Eighth's prominent air leaders; Capt Fred Castle, who would die leading my 487th Bomb Group on one of its most difficult missions; and Capt Beirne Lay Jr. who commanded my 487th when the group flew its first combat mission on 7 May 1944. Rounding out the staff were Maj Peter Beasley, Lt Harris Hull and Lt William Cowart. Headquarters for the Eighth was established at High Wycombe – code name *Pinetree* – on 23 February 1942.

Eaker had no airplanes, yet in two years, as the Eighth approached maximum strength, there were 40 bomb groups and 16 fighter groups comprising it – a profound example of aircraft production and aircrew training in America's mobilization for the war effort. Most evident was that operational capability in the Eighth's wartime environment would never have happened without British active participation. Acquisition of land for and construction of airfields was provided by Britain, and obviously fundamental to Eaker's immediate needs. Initially, 75 airfields were realized in an area from London north to The Wash bay in East Anglia. Airfields for logistics and supply were also provided; two included depots for aircraft maintenance and overhaul – one in Northern Ireland and one at Warton near Liverpool. Airfield construction kept pace with the flow of aircraft and aircrews into England.

Lavenham

The airfields provided by Great Britain for the coming battle had the same characteristics, thus I offer one to illustrate both the airfield layout and the village environment in which it nested. Lavenham became the home of the 487th Bomb Group for over two years. The village lies between Suffolk's Bury St. Edmund and Sudbury, some ten miles south of Bury St. Edmund and about forty miles southeast of Cambridge. It is an ancient Suffolk village that grew out of the weaving trades accompanying Flemish settlers in the 15th century. In 1944 the architectural flavor of the village reflected this heritage, as indeed it still did in 1988 when I returned with my wife Sunny for the first time after the war. So many of the town's timbered, wattle, and daub structures go back to the middle of this millennium and perhaps earlier.

Saint Peter and Paul Church stands prominently on a hill overlooking the town, silently testifying to the economic richness brought to Lavenham by the weaving trades in those early times. Its imposing Gothic countenance seems more a cathedral than that of a country church. What fascinated me in 1944 was the sheer size of this structure in what seemed, through the eyes of a New Yorker, such a tiny village. As my flying experiences with the Eighth Bomber Command unfolded, the church tower – all 141 feet of it – would take on a seemingly non-Christian significance, not only for me but for the airmen like me who were so often found orbiting around Suffolk looking for their roosts. Returning from missions on several occasions in low visibility without electronic approach and landing aids, that tower became vital. Considering the number of airfields jamming East Anglia and the number of aircraft operating essentially in an uncontrolled air traffic environment, it does not take an Einstein to sense the chaos prevailing under marginal weather conditions. In 1944, the church tower served as a beacon for returning Lavenham aircraft. Today, Lavenham retains the essence of its ancient charm largely unchanged from the way I remember it. The village is now a very active tourist attraction.

The airfield that would serve as the home of the 487th Bomb

Group was designated as Station 137, located on farmland that nestled on the northwest side of the town, where several working farms were located within what became the airfield's perimeter. These farms and cottages were left intact, although the farmers were moved out because of security considerations. Farmers continued to work their fields as the airfield evolved. A large parcel of that land known as Lodge Farm was owned and operated by David and Beth Alston. Having been served notice that they would have to vacate their property, the Alstons succeeded in convincing the authorities (David said flatly, "I will not move") that they should continue to live at Lodge Farm and work around the base activity while tending their fields.

The Alstons took in the Americans as they would their own. In the years following the war, the Alston family was instrumental in making that surviving air base a monument to the men of the 487th. The Alston's surviving children have continued that tradition. Alston's grandson, John Pawsey, now operates Lodge Farm.

Construction of the air base began in late 1943. Three runways intersected, the longest of which, the east-west runway (09-27), was 6,000 feet. Runways were surrounded by a circular perimeter taxiway that led in turn to hardstands (or "buttons") where the group's seventy plus aircraft were dispersed when parked. Living sites, shops, and other support facilities were also dispersed within the farm complex. The airfield became operational in April 1944, and the 487th Bomb Group was in place at the airfield by mid-April. My squadron, the 837th, was in position when the Eubank crew (including me) arrived on 16 April.

837th Squadron: The Eubank Crew		
Pilot	2nd Lt Charles L. Eubank	
Copilot	2nd Lt Bernard T. Nolan	
Navigator	2nd Lt Frank W. Nelson	
Bombardier	2nd Lt David O. Wilcox	
Flight Engineer/Gunner	Sgt Harry E. Ferris	Top Turret
Radio Operator/Gunner	Sgt Robert E. Irving	Waist Gun
Gunner	Sgt Clifford B. Richer	Waist Gun
Gunner	Sgt Wilbur J. Pancoast	Ball Turret
Gunner	Pfc Lee Graham	Tail Turret
Gunner	Sgt T. A. Rivers	Nose Turret

Runways, taxiways, and hardstands were made of a bed of rubble taken from the bombed out areas of London, and over the rubble a layer of concrete was poured to get a stable surface. A carpet of macadam pavement was put down over the concrete.

Living areas were well dispersed with each of the four squadrons occupying its own living site comprised of groups of Nissan huts. The usual officers' club, theater, and medical, administrative, and technical facilities were strung along a road system that extended over a mile south of the runways and perimeter taxiway. The sprawl was enough to require at least a bicycle to get around. Most of us had bikes. They were issued to some of the key players, but I had to buy mine.

My 837th Squadron occupied Site 5, the site nearest the town of Lavenham, which we reached on foot over an ancient trail through the muddy fields that we called the "Burma Road." The Nissan huts, latrines, and orderly room were clustered near a road that connected the other living sites to the rest of the base. Each living site was equipped with slit trenches for air raid protection. The one night I recall that a German "intruder" made a run at the base, no one in our hut bothered to hit the slit trench.

Officers and enlisted personnel of the 837th squadron lived in separate huts, but all were in the Site 5 complex. Our hut housed the officers of the crews of Charles Eubank and Loye Lauraine, thus eight to the hut. There were no facilities for ablutions in the huts; these along with the latrines were in other nearby buildings. Eubank and Lauraine shared a small room near the entry end of the hut. The other six officers shared the common space. A tiny coal-starved heating stove centered in the common space was, to my knowledge, never lit during my tenure as a resident.

Eighth Bomber Command – Structure

The organizational structure of Eighth Bomber Command consisted of combat Air Divisions, Combat Wings, Bomb Groups and Squadrons. At peak strength each squadron had 18 aircraft and 18 aircrews to man them. Four squadrons comprised the group. Based on a strength report of 6 August 1944, there were 40 Bomb Groups organized in the First, Second and Third Combat Divisions. Among the three divisions were 14 Combat Wings with from two to five groups in each. First Division groups were all equipped with the B-17, the Second all B-24s; the Third was mixed with both B-24s and B-17s. In mid-July 1944, the B-24 groups of the Third Division were re-equipped with the B-17.

Buildup Begins

In the actual deployment scenario for Eighth Air Force bomber crews emerging from combat readiness training, most flew their newly assigned aircraft to the UK by two routes – the Southern Route via South America and Africa recovering initially in Northern Ireland, or the Northern Route via Goose Bay, Labrador, Iceland recovering at Prestwick in Scotland. From the recovery bases the crews flew directly to their new operating bases. Some sailed the briny.

The first bomb group, the 97th, arrived at RAF Polebrook on 9 May 1942. It flew its first combat mission with 12 B-17s on 17 August. The target was the Marshalling Yard at Rouen, France. This has always been regarded as the first combat mission flown by the Eighth Bomber Command. Col Frank Armstrong, one of the six with Eaker when he arrived in the UK in February, now commanded the 97th. A strong disciplinarian, he was sent by Eaker to replace Col Cornelius Cousland to reshape the loosely prepared 97th for combat. In his book *Twelve O'clock High*, Beirne Lay used the Armstrong image to build the character of Brig Gen Frank Savage, his fictional group commander. In Actuality, the first bombing strike by the USAAF occurred on 4 July, when six American crews from the 15th Bomb Squadron joined six RAF crews for an attack on German airfields in the Netherlands. RAF Douglas Bostons (Douglas A-20 Havoc) were flown by the American crews. The Fourth of July raid conceived by Hap Arnold was intended to deliver a morale-boosting message through the media. The 15th Squadron was re-deployed later to join the 12th Air Force in North Africa.

Through the balance of 1942 until year's end, Bomber Command began to build in strength: the 301st joined the 97th in September. In October the 92nd and 93rd, first of the operational B-24 groups, joined the mix. The 93rd flew its first mission on 9 October. In November the 91st came on board along with the second B-24 group, the 448th. The 303rd and 305th were added in November, and the 94th in December. In all, 25 missions were flown during the period against targets in France in the Low Countries, with concentration on submarine related targets. Losses were minimal – a deceptive number at best, considering what lay ahead. Escort fighters for these missions included Spitfires flown by American pilots and P-38s.

From these limited beginnings, the Eighth Air Force grew into its peak of organized air power – 40 bomb groups and 16 fighter groups – nearly 3,000 aircraft and aircrews comprising the epitome of air power for its era, to be known world-wide as "The Mighty Eighth."

Fighter Command

The Eighth Fighter Command was formed in February 1942. Maj Gen Frank O'Driscoll (Monk) Hunter was named its commander and set up shop along with Bomber Command at Bushy Park. Hunter was a veteran pilot with combat experience gained as a fighter pilot in WW I. He was an ace with nine victories, a Distinguished Service Cross with four Oak leaf Clusters and a French *Croix de Guerre* with palm. He led Fighter Command until May 1943 when Ira Eaker fired him for resisting modifications to the P-47 to increase its range. Eaker's intent was to incorporate two 108-gallon drop tanks under the wings. The P-47 then operational lacked the range needed for deep missions. Even with a single fuel tank slung beneath the fuselage the radius of action was insufficient for deep penetration to targets in Germany. Modification requirements also included increasing the fuel capacity in the wing tanks. With its eight .50 caliber machine guns in the wings, the P-47 packed a lethal punch, but configuration offered limited space for expansion and also posed structural considerations. Hunter's concern related to degrading performance.

The central, if not debilitating, issue the Eighth Air Force would face in its maturation was attrition that would by the end of 1943 reach unacceptable proportions. In the development phases of both the B-17 and B-24, air leaders were convinced that these aircraft could outrun and outgun conventional fighters. That view was promptly discarded with the advent of Spitfires, Hurricanes and Bf 109s, but the fix to the problem in the Eighth's combat environment was slow to unfold – and costly. Lacking were the fighter escorts needed by bombers when penetrating to targets deep in Western Europe. Arnold, Eaker, Doolittle, Hunter and Maj Gen Frederick L. Anderson – all were aware of the deficiency.

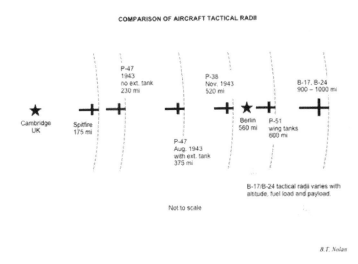

Figure 1

USAAF escort fighters at the outset included the twin-engine P-38, the P-47 and, for a limited time in 1942, the Spitfire, which was phased out to the disdain of many American fighter pilots. The Spitfire did not have the operating range for escort duty. Although well beyond the range of the Spitfire, the P-47 was limited even with one 108-gallon auxiliary fuel tank. As noted, modifications were made to install two external wing tanks, and by April 1944, the P-47 was escorting bombers on deep mission. The aircraft's high altitude capability gave it an edge in air-to-air engagement. When above an enemy aircraft, the P-47 could "bounce" the target and outrun anything in a dive to elude an attacker. Due to its size and weight, the P-47 has been characterized as vulnerable to the Bf 109 and FW 190 in a dog fight; however, kill scores attained by American fighter pilots suggest otherwise – that the bounce and run tactic prevailed. After the invasion, the P-47 proved to be a holy terror as a ground support weapon.

The multi-role P-38 had the required range with external fuel tanks installed; however, the aircraft had limits as a dogfighter. Its flight characteristics in air-to-air combat have been likened to those of Goering's Bf 110. The P-38 was no match to a Bf 109 or Fw 190 in air-to air combat. In any case, the solution to the escort issue lay ahead.

As the pounding of targets steadily increased in 1942, as well as the relentless growth of RAF and USAAF strike power, Adolf Galland, who commanded the Luftwaffe from 1941 to 1945, sensed the depth of the threat to German war production industries with one eye cast over his shoulder at what was happening on the Russian front. Galland was on the short end of the numbers, and he knew it. Both the British and American aircraft industries were now mass-producing bombers. Galland's strength would be augmented significantly in mid-1943 to meet what he anticipated was the budding capability of Eighth Air Force Bomber command, its threat to the industries of Germany, and the enormity of the air battle to come. Galland's defensive fighters in Western Europe were based in France and the Low Countries, organized in two *Jagdgeschwader*, or what we would call "wings." We knew them as the "Abbeville Kids" – young like us to be sure, but tough as nails and battle hardened. Unlike us, Galland's airmen had no respite from a defined combat "tour." They fought until they either died or the war ended. Like those of the Eighth Air Force and the RAF, their losses were appalling, yet another generation of young men sacrificed to appease the gods of war – and trashed by Hitler.

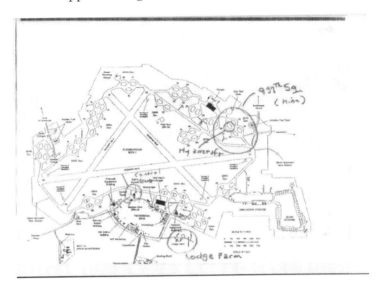

Station 137 Lavenham Airfield

Holness Collection

Black Double Chevron

P-47 Thunderbolt— "Razor Back"

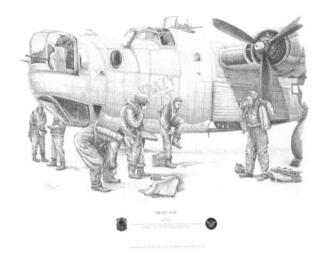

B-24 and Crew Preparing for Mission

B-17's in Good Formation
Photo Courtesy USAF Archive

97

CHAPTER 7   THE FORMATIONS

Formation structure and assembly were perhaps the most essential tactical ingredients that defined the Eighth Air Force Bomber Command's operational mode in the European campaign. Formations had to be assembled and flown in marginally acceptable weather, and indeed sometimes in unacceptable conditions. Pilots of the Eighth had to be able to maintain tight distances in relation to the aircraft leading the squadron or his element of three. As the campaign waxed on, variations in formation size and assembly techniques developed to hone precision and skills.

The process had little substance at the outset of operations in Europe because there were several dimensions to the problem of formation integrity. First, the structure of the formation had to be developed in consideration of both the optimum strike pattern and the best defense against fighters and flak. Second, the formation had to be "tight" with minimum maneuvering; i.e., shallow turns and very gradual altitude changes, if any, to make it flyable. Even greater stability was required on the bomb run to optimize the Norden bombsight's capability.

In an essay published in *Impact Magazine, Vol V*, General Curtis LeMay provided some graphic insights into the problem of formation integrity. When LeMay reached Prestwick, Scotland in November 1942 with his new 305th Bomb Group, he assembled his crews to hear input from a veteran of many combat missions. What they heard from the veteran painted a dark picture: "The flak is murder. If you fly straight and level for more than ten seconds, you're a dead duck." LeMay knew instinctively that if he could not fly straight and level for ten seconds, there was no way of hitting the target. Even under the best of circumstances in bomb-drop training exercises, such as we got in the Western desert, enough

99

time had to be provided in level flight to stabilize the gyro of the Norden sight, enter the speed information, and kill the drift. In actual combat operations, the evasive maneuvers were taken for survival – changing altitude and weaving turns; this erased any possibility of accuracy. Typical of LeMay, whom I regard as our most creative and aggressive air leader, he began chewing on the problem.

In *Impact* he writes, "I lay awake nights wrestling with the problem. Something was wrong – terribly wrong. Finally I had a brain storm just before our first mission against the sub pens at St. Nazaire, got out of bed, went to my foot locker and pulled out a copy of an old ROTC artillery manual and started scribbling figures. I based my calculations on probability of hits from a French 75-millimeter cannon on a target the size of a B-17 at a range of 25,000 feet, about right for Jerry flak gunners with their 88-millimeter flak batteries. The answer came out 273 rounds fired per hit on a B-17. By golly, I told myself, those are pretty good odds. I am going to try flying straight and level on the bomb run even if it takes minutes instead of seconds. Otherwise we might as well all stay at home."

LeMay's thinking on the probability of one hit in 273 anti-aircraft shells fired may have suited his reasoning process, but I think it was flawed. The German 88mm artillery piece was one of the war's most effective weapons, not only in the anti-aircraft mode for which it was originally designed, but for traditional infantry support barrages as well, and most especially as a tank killer. Its barrel could be depressed three degrees, elevated to 85, and traversed 360. It fired a 22-pound projectile at a rate of 15 to 20 rounds per minute and was effective vertically to a range of nearly 35,000 feet. A German city defended by as many as 400 guns firing 20 rounds per minute at a formation of 100 American bombers in guns' range for, say, 10 minutes could fill the air in the proximity of the formation with 80,000 88 mm fused shells. Dividing LeMay's number (273) into the 80,000 yields with a hit probability of 293 was totally unrealistic for an attacking force of 100 aircraft. His analysis was based on a different gun firing at a stationary target.

Hans Rumpf, citing official German sources in his book *The Bombing of Germany*, calculates that 3,343 shells fired would bring down one bomber. Using the same scenario, 100 attacking aircraft, 400 guns firing 20 rounds per minute for 10 minutes works out to a loss rate of 2.7 percent, which compares favorably with the table on page 76 entitled "Survival Odds for Eighth Air Force Air Crews." None of this takes into account bombers damaged.

In any case, LeMay's thinking set the pattern for the tactics that evolved. There would be neither altitude changes nor evasive turns on the bomb run between the "initial point" (IP) and the target, and the two were separated in terms of time by about ten minutes, to give adequate time for bombardiers to stabilize their Norden bombsights.

Improvement in formation structure with the development of the "combat box," also attributed to Curtis LeMay, was the very essence of both our offensive and defensive tactics. The basic concept of the combat box was to stack the aircraft vertically as opposed to horizontally, thus easing the problems of station keeping, especially in handling turning maneuvers. This box formation also yielded both good drop patterns and defensive firepower when attacked by enemy fighters. Even though Beirne Lay introduced us to the combat box during the late phases of our training in Alamogordo, New Mexico, we would not really become good at formation flying until well into the combat experience.

The basic formation structure from the outset was the three aircraft "V" (RAF's Vic) – also referred to as an element. A squadron, when assembled, regardless of size – i.e., six, nine, or twelve aircraft – was a gaggle of "Vs" in a stack. The squadron was the basic attack unit, flying to its assigned target as a unit and dropping bombs in unison. Three squadrons comprised the group attack force, and each group was assigned a specific target. There was a lead, a low, and a high squadron separated by about 500 feet in altitude with little separation in lateral distance; that is to say, laterally, the squadrons were also in a loose stack. On reaching the IP, each squadron peeled out of the group formation and made its separate bomb run to the target. After "bombs away," each squadron proceeded to the Rally Point (RP) where the group reassembled for the return leg to England.

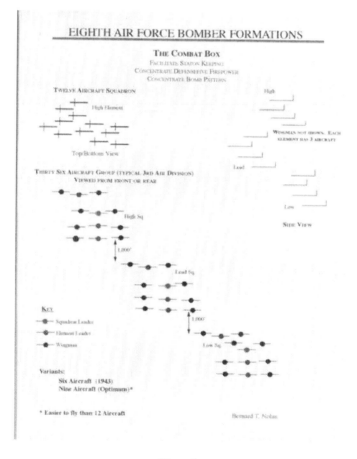

Figure 2

Six aircraft squadrons were common in the earlier days (1942-1943) of the Eighth's experience, three squadrons of six aircraft each for a total group strength of 18. As the bomber force grew to its peak, twelve aircraft squadrons prevailed, although there were many variations in size and structure in the three Air Divisions of the Eighth.

In April 1944, when I arrived in England, the common variant employed by the Third Air Division (then commanded by LeMay) was the 12 aircraft squadron with three squadrons comprising the group when assembled for a strike. Bear in mind, by mid-1944, as the Eighth Air Force Bomber Command reached its maximum strength of 40 bomber groups, each group had four squadrons, each composed of 18 aircraft and crews. Thus, the typical group never committed more than half of its strength to any single mission.

The overwhelming strength of the Eighth Bomber Command is readily apparent in these numbers. Multiply 40 times 4 times 18 and it yields 2,880 aircraft and crews. Even more amazing was the rate at which the build up of the strategic bombing force proceeded. The Casablanca Conference in February 1943 resulted in a call for 2,702 heavy bombers by March 1944 [see Chapter 5]. The influx of aircraft and crews into the air battle arena evolved essentially on schedule. Even by today's standards of management, this was an incredible feat of aircraft production, airfield construction, aircrew training, logistical planning, and execution. Raids on Continental Europe composed of 1,000 aircraft became routine by mid-1944, and they involved less than half the heavy bomber strike capability when launched. It is almost beyond comprehension to grasp the sheer magnitude of the strike force, let alone the problem of assembling squadrons, groups, wings, and divisions into a coherent attack force proceeding to selected targets in France, Germany and the Low Countries.

The true dimensions of this aerial armada hit me for the first time during one of my wartime visits to London. Early one fairly clear morning while walking near Hyde Park, my attention was drawn to the skies by the unmistakable drone of aircraft engines. Noise levels became more distinct and louder signaling the Doppler effect of oncoming aircraft – as one might liken to an approaching train. Several groups were proceeding in formation – both B-17s and B-24s at different altitudes. They were clearly visible through a thin layer of London haze as they passed directly overhead on a southeasterly track toward France, still climbing to assigned altitudes. Airspeeds appeared to be much slower than I expected from my street-level perspective. The procession seemed endless, continuing for a half-hour or so as the noise faded back to a drone and then disappeared. I became aware of the huge size of the bomber stream from the airborne perspective once or twice in the months following, but it was that London street scene that awakened me to the reality of what I was involved in.

When assembled for a strike, my 837th Squadron was composed of four elements of three aircraft. The second element leader flew under the tail of the squadron leader, and the third element leader under the tail of the number two leader. One additional threesome, called the high element, flew above and slightly to the right of the squadron leader. This was by far the most difficult position to fly in the process of maintaining good formation. For this reason I always thought the nine aircraft squadron was the optimum format. I flew these squadron formations both in the B-24H and the B-17G. The differences in the two aircraft were significant.

We worked our tails off flying those B-24 formations. Maintaining the essential tight formation was indeed quite a feat in the B-24, which taxed the best of us. Flying the wing position versus squadron or element lead was by far the most difficult. Constant aileron, rudder, elevator, and throttle inputs were required to maintain position on the wing, and the closer one tried to fly to the other aircraft, the more accentuated the movements became. Flying wing in the low element was the worst — call it the "crack the whip" effect. Seemingly minute and gentle corrections by the leader would be accentuated threefold by the time they reached the low element wing men. If ever there was a requirement for two pilots, it stemmed from the need to trade off stints at the controls while flying formation. It was difficult and tiring, far more so in the B-24 at high altitude than the B-17, I would learn. Flying the slot position under the squadron leader's tail was much less demanding. In this case, the pilot at the controls was looking directly up at the lead's tail turret. The squadron lead was the easiest position to fly, but the lead pilot had to maintain distances and altitudes relating to those of the other squadrons. The lead pilot, relying mostly on the automatic pilot for smoothness, had to be extremely gentle in course corrections, turning maneuvers, and altitude changes. Squadron and group lead pilots also had to be endowed with the courage to keep going through the fiercest of enemy fighter and flak attacks.

The higher the altitude, the more difficult it got because of the thinning air. One of our most common B-24 problems was engine failure, simply because we were beating them to death with the high power settings needed for operating at or above 20,000 feet.

The potential for collisions when flying in formation was high, and they were not at all uncommon. There were many other terrifying aspects. Flying into cloud decks was the surest way to break up a squadron formation, even more effective than German fighters. On several of the 33 missions I flew in both B-24s and B-17s, our squadron entered clouds in tight formation only to be scattered and dispersed. On the occasions this happened to us, we came out of enemy territory completely alone, once or twice with American or British escort fighters. Another facet of this problem not caused by weather patterns per se was the extensive contrails we generated. We were always running into the contrails and wakes of the formations ahead of us.

Assembling squadrons, groups, and wings, and then feeding them into the bomber stream was accomplished either visually over the airfield in good weather conditions or by using homing beacons in conjunction with the airborne radio compass in poor or marginal conditions above the clouds.

In the visual assembly procedure, the squadron leader took off and climbed on a straight ahead course at 150 mph indicated air speed (IAS), with a rate of climb about 400 feet per minute. After two minutes, the lead pilot would establish a shallow left turn. His right wing man would take off 30 seconds later and establish a left turn with his nose well within that of the leader to facilitate closure. When nearing the lead aircraft in this catch up maneuver, the right wing man would slide under the leader and take his position on the right wing. The third aircraft would follow the second by 30 seconds setting up a left turn inside the leader's nose and take his position on the left wing. The fourth aircraft would follow suit and take the slot position under the lead aircraft's tail. And so on until all 12 aircraft were in position. The lead aircraft would then take the assembled squadron to a higher altitude and a rendezvous point while awaiting the assembly of the second and third squadrons. Assembled groups would rendezvous over homing beacons or some geographical fix before setting course for their targets at precise time assignments.

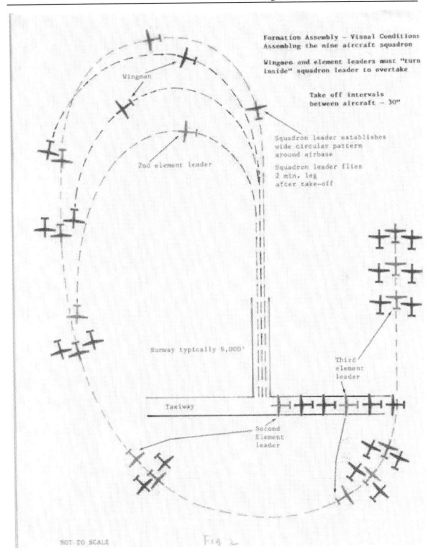

Figure 3

Because of marginal weather, often visual assembly became more the exception than the rule as the campaign moved along. In fact, I can't remember forming up visually for a mission more than half a dozen times.

In 1942 and 1943, the main problem in maintaining the continuity

107

and flow of bomber strikes against enemy strategic targets was the weather. During the winter months of 1942-1943, Eighth Air Force operations were slowed considerably by either poor weather for the assembly or over the target area. Some bad weather assemblies were attempted using simple dead reckoning procedures to reach assigned assembly points. The results were chaotic.

At the time, the RAF was operating medium frequency homing beacons called Splashers for aircraft orientation and recovery. Splashers were on line for daily operations, and they used pre-arranged frequencies and call signs to preclude jamming or "keying" (overriding a Splasher's broadcast signal to lead aircraft astray). The Eighth Air Force initially used these beacons as rendezvous points for group and wing assembly. Later in the campaign, however, they were used for assembling squadrons above cloud cover.

In October 1943, additional low powered, low frequency beacons called Bunchers were added to some 24 sites near operational Eighth Bomber Command airfields. Bunchers had an effective range of about 25 miles. A Buncher would typically be assigned to a combat wing for assembling its component groups at different altitudes.

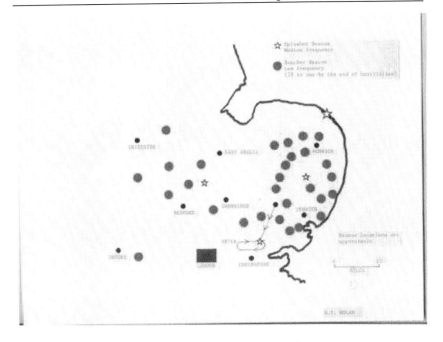

Formation Assembly Above Clouds

Our 487th Bomb Group used a Splasher for assembly; it was located at Harwick, some 10 to 15 miles north of Chelmsford and about 20 miles south of our departure point at Lavenham. The squadron lead aircraft would take off and fly a southerly course using the automatic feature of his radio compass, tracking to and over the beacon. Wingmen would follow suit in 30-second intervals. Assembly altitude was pre-assigned, based on airborne weather reconnaissance, in advance of prescribed take-off times, thus we were fairly well assured that assembly could be accomplished in the clear. After passing over the beacon, the lead aircraft established a racetrack pattern in relation to the beacon, much as aircraft do today when ordered into holding patterns by air traffic controllers. The lead aircraft fired color-coded flares for identification. Turns were made to the left, and wing men assembled on the leader in elements in the same manner as they did in visual conditions over the airfield.

In this process, the lead squadron would hold while the other two squadrons formed over the same beacon at different altitudes. The assembled group would enter the bomber stream at the prescribed time and proceed to its assigned target.

All this discussion on formation structure and assembly is replete with very nominal values in terms of altitudes, distances, and timing. Murphy's law prevailed in 1944 as much as it does today; there were foul-ups galore. Our group CO Beirne Lay was late getting the 487th in the bomber stream on 11 May 1944, and while cutting corners during the flight in an effort to catch up, four aircraft were shot down, including Lay's. Aircraft often formed up on the wrong squadron. I did so twice that I remember. Mid-air collisions were common. I witnessed one during a poor visibility assembly while flying a B-17 in August 1944, and one involving a B-24 and B-17 occurred over our airfield the previous month. It was rare for anyone to survive those mid-airs.

There were several 487th practice missions involving assembly of a full size group attack force of 36 aircraft. I can remember flying only one of these – on 1 May 1944. The 487th was only one week from its first real combat mission and still woefully unprepared for what would come. This is the type of training we should have gotten before deployment to an operational theater of war. On this day, Chuck Eubank and I would once again have the opportunity to display our inexperience, only this time we edged a bit closer to "buying the farm."

There is an old saying in the flying business: "You may not know your density altitude, but your engine always knows." Without superchargers, the high operational altitudes that we had to reach would not have been attainable. Engine performance falls off markedly as an aircraft climbs, due to the change in density altitude. More simply put, the higher one goes, the less dense the air. Carburetors cannot perform with the same efficiency at, say,

5,000 or 10,000 feet as they would at sea level. Today, take-off performance for an aircraft without engine superchargers at Denver, Colorado's mile high airport, would require a longer ground run than it would at a sea level airport, because of the less dense air at Denver's elevation. Superchargers made their way into aviation technology to compensate for this phenomenon and to permit high altitude flight. Both the B-24 and B-17 aircraft I flew were equipped with electronically controlled turbine driven superchargers.

The B-24H and B-17G had turbo-supercharger controls that automatically synchronized engine manifold pressure settings of all four engines. The turbines of each engine were driven by exhaust gas from the collector ring. Turbine speeds were in turn controlled by a butterfly valve in the waste gate aft of the turbine. As the aircraft climbed to high altitude, engine manifold pressures were kept constant by the compressed air fed to carburetors by the turbines. Number 1 engine was run up prior to take-off, and the manifold pressure boost set at the appropriate 50 inches of mercury for takeoff, with a control knob on the pilot's side of the throttle quadrant. The waste gates of number 2, 3, and 4 engines would automatically track number 1. Manifold pressure on all four engines would remain at the required setting during the take off, climb, and at cruising altitude.

Formation flying, of course, demands constant power adjustments with throttles for station keeping. Both power changes and control inputs must be instantaneous. Flying tight formation was physically tiring and mentally demanding, and Eubank and I usually traded off after about twenty minutes at the controls. Both pilots had to be able to perform skillfully. Wouldn't it be cool, we thought, if throttle adjustments could be made with the supercharger control knob, thereby realizing profound savings in physical energy? Why didn't we think of this sooner? What we did not consider was the fact that power adjustments with the supercharger knob took a

111

fraction of time to register in the engines. Throttle adjustments, on the other hand, which we were used to, were instantaneous. Well, try it we did, and the result was almost fatal.

During the practice mission we were flying in our stack of 12 aircraft on the left wing of the second element lead when Eubank began the experiment. At first, it seemed to go well, but before long the power adjustments with the knob got well out of phase with what was delivered to the engines, and suddenly there was a power surge. About this time our squadron converged on another squadron entering the target area from our left at the same altitude. It was totally unplanned, and the result was the God-damndest gaggle of B-24s I ever saw, all contending for the same airspace. There were now aircraft on both sides – those of the 837th to our right and those of that renegade squadron boring in on our left. The coherence of both formations was utterly destroyed in a wild melee. As Eubank tinkered with the control knob, bringing on the unwanted power surge, we shot forward in the melee, overrunning aircraft on both sides. Chuck and I fought for the controls – literally. I had an aircraft on my side, and he was trying to avoid one on the left. Chuck instinctively initiated a right turn away from the danger on his side but into the aircraft on mine. I grabbed the control wheel and stopped the turn. I guess the upshot was that we negated each other's control inputs and somehow slid between the two aircraft popping out front with no contact, thank God. By this time B-24s were breaking

off in every direction. It was utterly miraculous that there were no collisions in that fouled-up process. Richard Gile, the only surviving pilot of the 837th Squadron with whom I have contact, flew the same practice mission. He describes the incident: "How well I remember slicing between the layers of big birds. That could have been the most humongous disaster of any single Eighth AF day."

No attempt was made to reform the squadron, and the mission obviously went belly up with a couple of dozen B-24s scattered all over East Anglia. Sheer panic – it was not the first time nor would it be the last my blood would surge in response to a pounding heart. Needless to say, we never attempted that flawed procedure again. From that point on when flying formation, our hands never left the throttles.

No Parachutes

Photo Courtesy USAF Archive

113

CHAPTER 8   THE UNFRIENDLY SKIES

As of early May 1944, I had yet to fly a single mission, but I knew full well that my combat contract was for 25, thus great speculation on the odds of survival invaded my thoughts. The 25-mission "tour" evolved in the two years prior to my arrival on the scene. On the surface it seemed reasonable enough, and in some ways I was grateful for the fact that there was a finite number of missions in the contract. Had I played out the numbers, I might have thought very differently. The retrospective assessment indicates that the 25 missions posed long odds that I would survive the tour without being killed, taken prisoner, or wounded. In 1943, when the Eighth Air Force was averaging losses of 8 percent per mission, it meant on the average that nobody could expect to finish the tour. Losses of 100 percent would occur at 12.5 missions. In my case, the 1943 odds scenario worked fairly accurately; my head was almost blown away on my 14th mission, and I was shot down on my 19th.

Survival Odds for Eighth Air Force Air Crews
Theoretical Mission Tour 25
4% Loss Rate: No one completes 25 missions
2% Loss Rate: 50-50 chance of finishing 25 missions
Early 1943 Loss Rate 8%: No one completes 13 missions

Losses decreased steadily as tactics improved through intense training, the development of the combat box formation, and long range fighter escort. Except for the first four months of 1944, Eighth Bomber Command losses gradually decreased as air superiority gravitated to our side. Heavy losses continued early that year, when on March 6th, 69 aircraft went down on the Eighth's first Berlin raid. Six more were written off and 347 suffered damage. Considering the number of bombers dispatched – 730 – March 6th was no picnic. Thirty-seven bombers went down over Berlin on March 8, and eight more on the 9th. P-51 escorts flew in support on all three Berlin raids. By May 1944, when the new 92nd Bomb Wing (486th and 487th groups) went into action, the situation began to change, as the P-51 and its emerging capability to provide long-range escort protection for the bomber streams became a major factor in the battle.

No sooner had I arrived on the scene than the mission tour was increased to 30. Reflecting on the situation now reminds me of the bombardier Yossarian in Joseph Heller's *Catch 22*. As he drew within a few missions of the magic number, it was increased. Like Yossarian, every time the number increased, I felt like I had been shafted. The tour went from 25 to 30, and then 30 to 35 with an added wrinkle that we had the option to go home at 30 missions, if we agreed to return for a second tour. Many opted to do so, which made organizing complete crews for missions a nightmare for the squadron operations officers, especially in September 1944 when surviving crews were approaching the ends of their appointed tours. If I had played out some of those 1943 numbers with today's sensibilities, I probably would have run like hell. Naiveté may have blunted the reality of the peril, but I knew what I was up against. For me, and I think most, the frame of mind that would evolve related more to the idea of surviving from mission to mission than any other conscious thoughts. It also became very impersonal. I did not want to know who lived or died or who the replacement crews were, and I became more and more withdrawn.

There were so many ways to die other than in actual combat. Mid-air collisions were common. On 20 July 1944, two of our 487th aircraft collided over the base during a practice exercise to check out radar bombing equipment. I witnessed one during formation assembly in August of 1944. Awesome – the orange fireball spit forth large aircraft chunks, while several smoke plumes trailed as the fiery pieces plummeted toward English farm fields below. Accidents occurred all over East Anglia. Some guys bought the farm having what they thought was great fun buzzing various objects on the ground. Don't get me wrong; I had done my share of buzzing in cadet training when I knew I could get away with it, but I quickly learned what a real buzz job was all about.

Buzzy Buzman (the name is fictitious; the anecdote following is true) was by far the hottest pilot in the 837th Squadron – just ask him! Buzman had a passion bordering on obsession for flying low, and did so every chance he got. He volunteered for all local test hops and training exercises in those pre-combat days of April 1944. I was drafted into service as his copilot for a B-24 test flight, following an engine change on April 22. The test flight took over an hour. At the end, Buzman hit the deck after a long, accelerating dive, and dragged that B-24 toward the base across the fields, skimming buildings, hurdling trees, and anything else in his path. After a low pass over the active runway, he pulled up sharply in a chandelle and came back down for more. Gravity forces plastered me into the seat during the pull up. Then as the speed bled away, I was weightless as we went over the top, near stall speed and into the next dive. As the saying goes, it was time for white knuckles and a pounding heart. At first I thought I was having fun, but it soon became apparent that Buzman was absolutely psychotic about how close he could come to various ground objects without hitting them. It might not have been so bad if I had been at the controls, but it was Buzman's hands, feet, and goofy mind that guided the aircraft. All I could do was sit there and squirm, trying to will the next pull up before Buzzy actually applied back pressure on the control column to escape some object – always at the last microsecond. Good Jesus, deliver me from this maniac. By the time we entered the traffic pattern for a normal approach and landing, I was tight as a drum. As we came in on the final approach, my feet were up on the rudder pedals. When we touched down, Buzman went absolutely ballistic: "Don't you ever touch those God-damned controls when you are flying with me unless I tell you." I was out of the seat before the aircraft rolled to a stop. "Don't worry, Buzzy, you won't ever have to fly with me again, and you can stuff this B-24 and both rudder pedals up the farthest reaches of your ass." In fairness, Buzman later sought me out after the flight to apologize. It was the last time we talked.

A few days later, Buzman was handed another test flight, this time without a copilot. I doubt that anyone wanted to be with him on those local flights. Word spreads fast. He recruited a sergeant from the squadron operation's office as copilot, and the latter took his place in the right seat. Buzman came over our living site and began one of his signature low passes, pulled up, then made another low pass from a different direction, and another – each one lower than the last. His final pass was at roof level over our huts and toward a copse of trees bordering a field on the fringe of the hut area. It was those trees that would end Buzman's buzzing career and claim his life, as well as that of the sergeant "copilot" who was unfortunate enough to be in the right seat. Beyond the trees there was the usual fireball, and that was that. Scratch one B-24H, one aircraft commander, and one operations sergeant.

Richard Gile, fellow 837th Squadron survivor writes: "How well I remember Buzman's fatal mistake. Our hut was at the end of the complex, and for a few scary seconds it looked like he wasn't going to clear it. When he pulled up, he mushed, and it's not clear whether it was the tail or the prop wash that knocked off the stick we had on the end of the hut for an antenna wire. The trees beyond the base weren't as forgiving in his next pull-up attempt. As I remember, it was the Squadron Operations Sergeant who was with him. We heard that they paid the sergeant's insurance, because he could have been ordered on the flight, but not Buzman's, because of his gross negligence, which lost an aircraft. Can't vouch for the last, but the heart stopping miss of the hut is unforgettable."

The early missions we flew brought many new enemies into our lives – all seemed intent on killing us. To be sure, flak, fighters, and the intricacies of the formation were all bad enough, but there were other factors that need some attention if I am to adequately portray the aerial combat environment during WW II in Europe. One was fatigue. Another was the effect on the body of the extremely low temperatures at high altitude. Wake turbulence encountered in formation was still another. Of these, pilot fatigue was the most dangerous. And there was also bleeding to death from untended wounds, anoxia from oxygen system failure, or at the hands of irate German civilians if brought down.

Most of my 33 missions began very early in the day. Wake up call came about 3:00 a.m. with take off at first light, or sometimes before dawn, which appeared early considering the higher latitude of England. I was there during the high sun months just before and after the summer solstice.

We usually knew when a mission was laid on the group the night before. Remember the "Toby Mug" in Beirne Lay's *Twelve O'clock High*? In the film, the mug resided on the fireplace mantle in the officers' club of this fictional bomb group. Whenever the group was alerted for a mission the next day, the group executive officer (Dean Jaeger) would quietly go to the mug and turn its face to the wall. All the flying officers, seeing the mug reversed, would dutifully disengage from the bar and return to their quarters. That tale either started with Lay's fictional bomb group or found its way into the 487th group's lore sometime after the war. The story of the mug persists, and at a reunion of the 487th veterans in Lavenham in 1995 there was a ceremony relating to the mug at what remains of the fireplace in the old officers' mess. I remember the alerts well, but cannot remember ever seeing the mug. Lay didn't last long enough with the 487th to really give that tale any substance, but it does make a nice story.

Anticipating the mission when we knew it was on made sleeping difficult at best. Fear became a regular visitor of the night. Minds would begin playing games with target location, usually in prayer for a "milk run," a euphemism for an easy mission. Better yet, maybe an aircraft would get shot up enough to have to recover in Sweden or Switzerland. If that happened, the crew would be interned. What a great way to sweat out the war – guaranteed survival.

Life in those Nissan huts was difficult even without the mission alert, leaving us in a constant state of fatigue. The officers of two crews shared our hut, eight of us raucous guys under one roof. It was commotion that ruled the roost in that hut. Long periods of deep sleep were always rare and cherished when such opportunities surfaced. If we got to sleep by midnight, being awakened at 3:00 am made us zombies before the day even started.

It seemed like Chuck Eubank and I were always tired. By the time we were airborne, deep fatigue was already setting in. Nodding off in a formation was a sure ticket for an interview with St. Peter. When assembled in the pack with the rest of the squadron, even trading the controls every twenty minutes was not enough, and exhaustion seemed ever there, pervasive and, like Homer's sirens, always luring us to Morpheus. Nodding off when not at the controls was frequent, and by mid-mission my mind began to wander into a kind of subconscious reverie. With concentration so often broken by the little catnaps, I can remember getting to the point during the flight where I didn't give a damn.

The worst day for me was 20 June 1944, when we flew two missions, one to the Hanover/Misburg area. The second mission target was the shorter of the two and therefore probably to a German airfield in France or Belgium. I was in the air for eleven hours that day. I recall the first briefing around midnight and take off in the darkness with just a hint of twilight on the eastern horizon. It was about 4:00 a.m., the day before the solstice. Returning from the first flight, the second briefing was about 1:00 p.m., and we returned to Lavenham in the absolutely last streak of twilight. It may have been close to 11:00 p.m., possible considering the "double British summer time" during the war years. The British set their clocks forward by two hours. When we landed at Lavenham following the second mission, I was a basket case, so tired that I had to be helped from the aircraft.

Another enemy was the cold. It is truly difficult to characterize the misery associated with high altitude flight in an unheated aircraft. I say unheated even though the B-24H did have a very small gasoline-fed heater on the flight deck. There may have been one or two others forward of the waist position, but that is irrelevant since the heaters were utterly useless.

In the month of May, air temperatures in England vary quite a bit, but in 1944 there was nothing extreme I recall either toward warm or cold days. On a balmy day with the mid-day temperature running about 60° Fahrenheit (about 15° Centigrade) at the surface, temperatures at 20,000 feet in a "standard atmosphere" would be -13° Fahrenheit, or -25° Centigrade.

We would usually be at our aircraft about an hour before the scheduled "start engines" signal from the tower, sitting around under the wing – waiting. Based on what we had to wear, plus the temperature variances at ground level and high altitude, the discomfort factor would be enormous.

Flying clothing issued to us for those missions in May 1944 consisted of wool-lined sheepskin jackets, trousers, boots, and a helmet. Goggles were provided with the helmet, but never pulled down over the eyes, contrary to aerial combat scenes in many Hollywood films. They were there to protect the eyes from fire and to enable unimpaired vision in the event of a shattered windshield. The main function of the helmet was to anchor the oxygen mask without which one could not survive at high altitude.

Throat microphones were issued to enable intercom and air/ground radio transmissions. These were essential when oxygen masks were in place over the nose and mouth, denying the use of standard hand-held microphones. They consisted of two microphone pick up sensors residing on either side of the Adam's apple and held in place with a neck strap.

Flotation vests ("Mae West") and parachute harnesses were worn over the sheepskins. I usually wore coveralls over my regular uniform trousers, foregoing the sheepskin trousers, but I wore the jacket. A chest pack parachute mated with the quick release harness, which facilitated easy escape when landing, but the pack itself had to be stowed behind our seats. I would have much preferred the back pack type parachute. If one were blown out of the aircraft, which did happen, at least the pack would be there. Flak vests were also issued to us, but Eubank and I did not wear them, preferring instead to spread them out on the flight deck. I remember a mission when a visiting dignitary from upstairs in the group's hierarchy boarded our aircraft as an observer. He was indeed very thankful for our unworn flak vests. He climbed on that flak vest sanctuary as soon as we entered enemy territory and never budged until we left, "observing" little or nothing. At least he got credit for flying a mission.

On a 60° F day, all this stuff could not be donned until just minutes before getting the "go" signal, at which time we entered the aircraft and began going through the check lists in preparation for starting engines. By the time engines were running and the aircraft was in the taxi line to the active runway, crewmen were already sweating in that heavy gear. After take off and on the ensuing climb and assembly, the sweating got only worse, at least for the pilots, as they horsed those controls in the process of formation flying. By the time 20,000 feet and those sub-zero temperatures were reached, the cold began to penetrate through those now wet undergarments. When not at the controls I remember stamping my feet for circulation and trying to get my gloved hands under my armpits to warm them, but there was no way to warm the body. Frostbite was a common problem for airmen of the Eighth Air Force.

During the sweating phase of this experience, moisture always built up in our oxygen masks, seeping through the air discharge vent in the mask and collecting as ice on our scarves. Chuck and I usually had small beads of ice on our chests just below the mask. I always thought we looked like a pair of drooling babies. Chapped necks dogged us daily. Neck irritation was further exacerbated by our throat mikes which had to be pressed against the Adam's apple with fingers of a free hand when transmitting. I wore an olive colored lamb's wool scarf to try to protect my neck, with some success. The whole experience was pervasively miserable, but had to be endured until the aircraft descended into the warmer air on the homeward leg of the mission.

The advent of the heated flying suit was our salvation. These were issued to us some time in June 1944. The heated suit consisted of a wired foot liner that fit inside the sheepskin lined boot, and a wired body liner that was worn under a dark green gabardine jacket and trousers. The jacket was cut in the style of the British "battle jacket" (or Eisenhower, if you like). No insignia was worn. Suits were designed intentionally not to look like uniforms in order to facilitate evading the Germans if we were brought down. But they were uniforms nonetheless, and I am sure the Germans recognized them as easily as we did. The heated undergarment elements were plugged into a 115 Volt AC power source in the aircraft that had a rheostat for controlling the heat levels. The heated suit worked well for me.

Another threat to survival was wake turbulence from the groups ahead, which could make tight formation flying an absolute nightmare. Imagine the swirling vortices churned up by a thousand propellers and wing tips somewhere ahead and the turbulence associated with them. The chop was often unmanageable. A pilot would be flying along with his wing tip tucked tightly on the element leader. Suddenly that wing tip would get hung in a vortex, conveying the notion that it was stuck in glue without the immediate response a pilot expects from aileron control inputs. Rigorous rudder, elevator, and throttle corrections were required to avoid mid-air collisions in such instances. It was debilitating and, to me, sometimes a poor trade for the flak and enemy fighters. Suffice it to say, beyond the Germans, we had a multitude of enemies bent on our destruction.

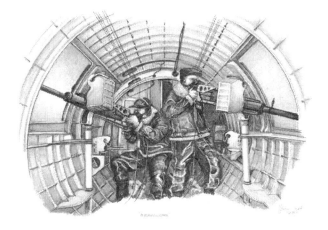

Aluminum Cages

CHAPTER 9   THE ALUMINUM CAGES

On the eve of our entry into the combat arena, our ten-man crew was beginning to bond as a unit. The thin line separating officers and enlisted men in the airmen's world became obscure at best, even though there was very little social interaction in our lifestyles or day-to-day activities. We lived in separate huts and ate in different mess facilities, except for a brief interlude when we tried out a single mess hall for all combat crewmen.

The adhesive that held diverse personalities together as crews was the common danger they faced – they depended on each other – a very common element in soldiering. In reflection, I marvel at the courage our crewmen displayed in repeatedly entering the airborne death traps they had to occupy during those missions. All of the crew positions one might man in either the B-17 or B-24 were fraught with danger in time of peril. The nose section of the B-24 housed both pilots, the radio operator (who also manned a waist gun when under attack), and the engineer-gunner on the flight deck with the navigator, bombardier, and nose gunner up front. The escape route for the latter three was through the nose wheel doors. An emergency lever in the vicinity of the nose wheel hatch opened the doors but left the nose wheel in the retracted position. The pilot, co-pilot, radio operator, and flight engineer evacuated through the bomb bay. An emergency lever on the flight deck within the pilot's reach opened the doors and simultaneously released any bombs still in their racks. These crewmen had to get out of their seats, retrieve chest parachute packs, snap them in position on the harness, and then get to the entry door from the flight deck to the bomb bay. Try that some day with about six times the force of gravity anchoring your feet as though in slabs of concrete.

Consider the plight of the gunners. Of the turret positions, the bottom fuselage "ball" was by far the most dangerous. The Sperry ball turret in the B-24 was retractable, anchored to the top of the inner fuselage and raised by hydraulic pressure. It lowered itself when the pressure was released, but this mechanical abomination had to be aligned for either entry or egress. Getting one in and out of the ball turret required help, and when inside, the occupant was in the fetal position with his knees under his chin for hours on long missions, with twin 50s recoiling within inches of his head whenever fired. In time of trouble with the aircraft gyrating or in a dive, there was no way to get out of that human fire trap.

The ball turret in the B-17, fixed in the down position, was even more dangerous than that of the B-24. There is at least one case on record where the ball gunner in a B-17 was trapped in his turret due to battle damage. The turret was frozen in a position where it could not be aligned properly to open the exit door. Worse, on return the crew could not get the landing gear down and had to make a belly landing. The gunner was crushed to death. Nose and tail turrets in the B-24 were not much better, with sliding doors both requiring alignments for entry and departure. If these rotating turrets could not be properly aligned due to battle damage or mechanical failure, there was no way to get the gunner out. The top fuselage turrets in both aircraft were reasonably comfortable, in comparison to the others, and much easier to enter and leave. The waist gun positions were the most comfortable. Waist gunners could sit or stand and move about for other chores such as dispensing chaff. But the waist position could also be deadly if an aircraft experienced a spin, flat out dive, or any other out of control situation in which centrifugal force could immobilize the entire crew. In such situations, non-anchored items such as flight bags, ammunition boxes, gun casings, parachute packs, or whatever else was about, could pummel waist gunners. In a dive, the waist gunners would wind up on the aft bomb bay compartment wall — now the floor — some ten feet from their waist window escape route. The alternative was to get out through the bomb bay, providing the doors were open. In such situations there was no way to help the ball turret gunner. Our gunners who flew these positions all knew this, and they faced bravely – as we all did – the reality of being trapped.

Col Beirne Lay Jr. took command in February 1944 during the later stages of the group's combat training at Alamogordo, New Mexico. Before the war, Lay was a writer by trade. He wrote several screenplays dealing with military aviation, including a priceless piece of work for a film called *I Wanted Wings*. Lay was a reserve officer, and he trained as a pilot in the 1930s. Lay was also a hands-on leader who had pledged in a speech to the assembled group in a hangar at Alamogordo that he would fight not only for us but also with us. He made good on that pledge. Lay was on his second major assignment with the Eighth. He was with Eaker at the very beginning. Eaker knew of Lay's background and assigned him initially as the command's historian. But Beirne Lay also flew some missions including the infamous Regensburg-Schweinfurt raid.

On 11 May 1944, Lay was shot down in the lead aircraft over an airfield near Châteaudun, France. The target that day was the railroad-marshaling yard at Chaumont, France. As noted earlier, Lay's timing was off, and the group had gotten behind in the bomber stream. In an effort to catch up, Lay cut some corners that took him over the heavily defended German airfield at Châteaudun. The 487th took a sound thrashing: four aircraft were lost to the German flak batteries at Châteaudun, including the one in which Lay occupied the copilot's seat as the mission commander. The pilot of the aircraft in which Lay led the group was 1st Lt. Frank Vratny. Lt Walter Duer was Vratny's co-pilot, but since Lay occupied the copilot's seat, Duer was positioned in the tail turret. All of Vratny's crew managed to bail out of the burning aircraft.

In his book *I've Had It*, Beirne Lay graphically describes his experience in baling out of a doomed B-24. When the evacuation order was given, Lay grabbed the emergency bomb release handle installed in the flight deck floor near the copilot's seat which he occupied. When the handle was pulled, the bomb bay doors were designed to open, release the bomb load and at the same time provide an evacuation route for those on the flight deck. He recounts: "I got the handle to move a few inches, but it jammed – the doors remained closed. I scrambled out of the copilot's seat, planted both feet on the floor and with both hands on the emergency release pulled mightily, but it would not budge." His only means of a quick exit was gone.

With the aircraft in a steep spiraling dive, Lay turned from the bomb bay and inched his way forward beneath the cockpit floor leading to the nose compartment where the nose wheel door escape opening was located. The nose wheel doors were opened in emergency for egress from that compartment, however, the nose wheel unfortunately remained stuck in the retracted position. The navigator, bombardier, and nose gunner used this opening for evacuation. Each had to make his escape by slipping by the retracted nose wheel. All three crewmen had already baled out when Lay got there. He recounts: "As I squeezed past the nose wheel my parachute harness caught something, and I was unable to make it through the opening." Lay says that "he felt helplessly trapped, and all hope left him." He fought clumsily to release himself and ultimately broke free. Finally, he says: "I wormed my way desperately toward daylight, and the suction caused by the slipstream rushing over the open hatch literally pulled me out of the aircraft. I yanked the ripcord as I left." His aircraft was seconds from impact.

Two other B-24s went down in flames over Châteaudun. Edward Brodsky piloted one of these. There were only three survivors, including Brodsky. The third, piloted by 2nd Lt Lorin McCleary, took a direct hit and exploded. There was only one survivor: S/Sgt Harold Owens was somehow blown clear in the explosion and captured by the Germans – perhaps the first of our POWs. Of the four aircraft lost, one was nursed back to England, but its flight ability deteriorated to the point that the crew abandoned it over the southeastern coast, where it crashed. All of the crewmembers survived the experience.

Lorin McCleary's wife was five months pregnant at the time of his death. Half a century later I would meet McCleary's, son who was named at his birth for the father he would never know.

The Germans never caught Lay. Under the aegis of the French underground, he hid on a French farm with his co-pilot, Lt Walter Duer, until American forces swept through the area and liberated him on 14 August 1944. In the meantime, Lay was replaced with a full colonel named Robert Taylor.

Nobody Got Out of That One
Photo Courtesy USAF Archive

CHAPTER 10   THE CARNAGE OF 1943

We new airmen emerging from training had an inkling of reality but no true insights into what was going on in the skies over Europe. To a great degree, our propaganda mills blinded us. I am reminded of an old canard from my NASA days: we called it mushroom management – "keep them in the dark and sprinkle some manure on them from time to time." That was the drill throughout my cadet training from February through October 1943. But reality was beginning to dawn on me as the true dimension of our losses began to filter through.

A hell of a lot was happening in Europe. The CBO campaign launched against the Axis was going full tilt when I emerged from pilot training in November. The daylight component of the CBO was entering a critical stage of its development.

Throughout the first half of 1943, the RAF carried the CBO load as the USAAF forces built up. Bombing tactics employed by both air forces were markedly different, as we have seen in Chapter 4.

USAAF and RAF strategists and mission planners considered air supremacy as their prime goal. A directive issued on 10 June 1943 called for a combined RAF/Eighth Bomber Command offensive in a series of strikes against 76 targets in six target systems, theorizing that such wholesale attacks were essential to destroying German fighter aircraft strength. Germany's Luftwaffe was to be destroyed in the air, on the ground, and in the factories.

Weapons and tactics employed by both the Allies and Germans throughout 1943 went through several innovative changes driven by the demands of combat. At the outset, American air leaders held on to the idea that the heavily armed and armored B-17s and B-24s could take care of themselves under any circumstances –

without escort fighters. These heavy bombers carried up to thirteen 50-caliber machine guns. In squadron stacks of 12 aircraft, they could fill the sky with lead for about a 1,000-yard cone of protection around the formation. Put two more squadrons in the stack to form an attacking group of 36 and you get an idea of what the Germans had to penetrate to get at us. The Germans countered with the use of rocket armed, twin engine Bf 110s that could sit well behind the range of the bombers' firepower and lob their explosive shells into the formations with deadly effect. The 20 mm cannons used by Luftwaffe fighters were equally deadly in destructive power. To a great extent we were out-gunned. Head-on fighter attacks were used as a tactic aimed at breaking up the formations. A well-aimed 20 mm shell could take out everybody in the nose of the bomber including both pilots. If the formation could be dispersed, its bombers could easily be picked off one by one. German anti-aircraft artillery flak concentrations and techniques using the 88-millimeter gun grew relentlessly. Flak concentrations around cities coupled with excellent day fighters and search radars countered the bomber's defensive capabilities more than adequately.

As the Eighth Bomber Command built up steadily during 1943, daylight raids increased both in frequency and numbers of aircraft committed. Penetration distances also increased. The USAAF would cling to the precepts of precision visual bombing based on accuracy attainable with the Norden bombsight. By year's end, however, the future of daylight bombing for raids against strategic targets deep in Germany was in serious doubt because of unacceptable attrition, resulting mainly from the lack of escort fighters with adequate operating ranges and a decided misperception as to the effectiveness of on-board defensive armament.

November 1943 was a time of crisis for our daylight precision bombing campaign against the German war machine. Both the

132

Eighth and Fifteenth Air Forces were building up rapidly, exerting some muscle. As the campaign unfolded in 1943, the strike capability of the Eighth built steadily, but so did its losses. Our air leaders never wavered in their goal for an effective daylight, precision strike force, but they completely deluded themselves on actual results, especially when considering the high cost in terms of aircraft and crews. General "Hap" Arnold and Major General Ira Eaker both optimistically persuaded themselves that the Eighth's attacks were causing irreparable damage to the Luftwaffe and to German war industry. Call it the "public relations" air war akin to the body count obsession of the Vietnam War. The reality was that the claims of aerial gunners were overblown, and bombing results were grossly overestimated. Nor did our air leaders pay the price for their convoluted optimism – they were willing to accept the high casualties. We grubs in the air over Western Europe were left to pay the piper.

As losses mounted to unacceptable proportions, the reality began to sink in. The idea that bombers could take care of themselves defensively in deep strikes against German targets was no longer realistic. At this stage of the battle there was no fighter escort once the bombers left France and Belgium for targets in Germany. Moreover, rather than neutralizing the German aircraft industry with these daylight raids, the Luftwaffe actually increased in size and rose to the challenge with a vengeance. By the time of the second Schweinfurt raid in October 1943, the losses being dealt to the Eighth Bomber Command were now unacceptable. In the Regensburg-Schweinfurt raids of August and October, 120 bombers – with 1,200 airmen aboard – were lost, and an additional 306 heavy bombers returned with battle damage, and of these, eleven were written off. The following table addresses the number of aircraft returning to England with heavy damage.

Selected Missions in 1943					
Date	Target	Attacking Force	Aircraft Lost		Aircraft Damaged *
			Number	Percentage	
26 Feb	Wilhelmshaven	65	7	10.7	
18 Mar	Vegasack	97	2	2.0	24
17 Apr	Bremen	107	16	15.0	39
21 May	Wilhelmshaven	123	5	4.0	11
11 Jun	Wilhelmshaven	82	26	32.0	62
26 Jul	Hannover-Hamburg	199	24	12.1	89
12 Aug	Bochum-Bonn	243	25	10.3	172
17 Aug	Regensburg / Schweinfurt	315	60	19.0	172
14 Oct	Schweinfurt	229	60	26.0	145
* Includes those aircraft "written off" as non-repairable					

Regensburg-Schweinfurt

The Eighth Air Force was on its knees in the contest for air superiority, driven in the summer and fall of 1943 by escalating losses of men and aircraft. The 17 August Regensburg-Schweinfurt mission produced perhaps the most savage air battle of the war and it magnified the trend and the outlook.

The plan was to launch two combat wings – the First and the Fourth – against German ball bearing production plants in

Schweinfurt and the Messerschmitt 109 aircraft and engine factory in Regensburg. In the planning, timing was critical. The First Bombardment Wing, led by Brig Gen Robert Williams consisted of nine B-17 groups totaling 240 aircraft, located in the English Midlands. The Fourth Bombardment Wing, led by Maj Gen Curtis LeMay had seven groups, totaling 146 B-17s, located in East Anglia. Departure times were to be staged with the objective of diverting Luftwaffe fighter defensives. LeMay would launch first to the most distant Regensburg and recover in North Africa, absorbing the brunt of the Luftwaffe fighter attacks on the way in. Williams would follow along the same general vector, free from the full weight of Luftwaffe fighters now engaging LeMay.

What can go wrong will, as Murphy the lawgiver expounded in his epic philosophical treatise. Weather conditions at the Midlands where Williams was located deteriorated to the extent that Major General Frederick Anderson, now head of Eighth Bomber Command, was confronted with a dilemma. He had three options: cancel the mission – losing ideal weather conditions over the continent and North Africa; send both forces at the same time; or send LeMay off on time waiting for weather at Williams' bases to clear. Anderson opted for number three, resulting in a delay of three and a half hours before Williams could get airborne. Option three turned out to be the worst choice as the operation unfolded. Luftwaffe fighters were afforded time for to attack LeMay's force, and then they could land, re-arm, and regroup for concerted attacks on Williams both on the way in and way out. The toll was terrifying: Williams lost 36 bombers, three airmen known killed on surviving aircraft, 12 wounded, and 352 missing. Most of the latter would become German prisoners. LeMay lost 24 aircraft, four known dead, 9 wounded, and 200 missing

Twenty-six percent of our bombers, the highest Eighth Air Force loss rate at the time, fell to the guns of well-coordinated attacks by Bf 109s, Bf 110s, and Fw 190s – more than one out of four.

135

These are absolutely appalling numbers. Beirne Lay describes the most vivid account of this mission in Roger Freeman's epic work, *The Mighty Eighth*. Lay, in a ringside seat, tells an incredible story that serves today as a centerpiece of aerial combat literature. The full text of Lay's essay is in Freeman's book, from which I offer the following:

Lay was in the co-pilot's seat of the aircraft leading the second element of the high squadron of the 100th Bomb Group (The Bloody Hundredth, it would be called), one of a column of the 16 groups comprising the force attacking Regensburg. The 100th, as well as the others, were under constant fighter assaults for over an hour after crossing the coast of the Netherlands. Lay likens going through the ensuing fighter attacks as a nightmare surpassing fiction – "running a gauntlet of spiked clubs," as he put it.

Ten minutes after making landfall, swarms of Bf 109s and Fw 190s rose to intercept them. Lay describes the attacks on his formation "as coming from all quadrants – head on, both flanks and the rear." Tactics employed by the Germans ran true to form. Head-on attacks were pressed with fighters either flying through the formations or executing a "split S" and breaking away with their bottoms up underneath his formation after firing their 20 mm canons and machine guns. Lay records, "with every gun on every B-17 firing, the air was filled with tracers to match those of the attacking fighters." Lay's B-17 shook from the action of its flexible waist guns and turrets, "and the aircraft filled with the odor of burning cordite. Bright orange funeral pyres of stricken bombers and fighters stretched out on the earth's green carpet marked the trail of the battle."

Both sides were hurt in this initial clash. Several B-17s fell in flames from the formations. Lay watched as two fighters exploded beneath him. The battle debris through which he flew – "shining objects were pieces of aircraft" – awed Lay. A large dark form passed through the formation, barely missing several propellers. It was a man with his knees clutched under his chin in the fetal position as he tumbled out of view. Lay was concerned over the threat to his aircraft posed by the airborne flotsam. Emergency hatches, exit doors, premature parachutes, bodies, and assorted aircraft junk comprised the debris chain. Lay watched as crewmen from stricken B17s struggled to get out: "A B-17 copilot squeezed through his side window, reached back for his parachute, clamped it in place, and let go. The horizontal stabilizer hit him. The parachute never opened." Lay's attention was drawn to another burning B-17 as it dropped away from the formation. While still in a straight and level attitude about 200 yards from Lay, seven of the crew bailed out successfully. He did not see the pilots leave. Minutes later, the B-17 passed from view in a sheet of yellow flame.

Once through the peak intensity of the fight, the savagery of the air battle became apparent. Disintegrating aircraft were everywhere in the scene, and Lay noted "sixty parachutes visible in the air at any given look. The yellow parachutes were Germans, the white ours."

The 100th Bomb Group had been under attack for a solid hour, and the target was still thirty-five minutes distant. Seven of the group's 21 aircraft had been shot out of the sky. Lay thought the group would be annihilated.

Nearing the IP, an hour-and-a-half during which Lay estimated 200 individual fighter assaults took place, the attacks ceased. The remaining fourteen aircraft of the 100th Bomb Group turned at the IP and made their run at the target. Two of those, crippled in the action, fell out of formation after dropping their bombs and made their way to Switzerland. The rest of the group flew on south to recover in North Africa as planned, to complete the Eighth Air Force's first "shuttle" mission. Lay's aircraft was close to fuel starvation as it landed with "fuel warning lights glowing red." I have often wondered what might have happened to the remainder of the Schweinfurt strike force had they run the gauntlet of German fighters on a return to England through Germany instead of recovering in North Africa. The Luftwaffe's 109s and 190s would have been rearmed, refueled and waiting.

If there is a positive note in this mess it lies in the fact that Col Hub Zemke's P-47 escort fighters, at the limit of their endurance, made their appearance above Williams' formations near the German-Belgium border. Still without the range to reach Regensburg or Schweinfurt, the positive note is that the P-47 fared well against Galland's fighters. Zemke's P-47 shot down 11 Luftwaffe fighters at a cost of three P-47s.

On 6 September, Ira Eaker went after ball bearings again: this time Stuttgart was the target, again beyond the range of protective cover. One would think at this point a lesson would have somehow been driven home to Eaker and his planners, but Hap Arnold was in town and apparently the Eighth planners wanted to put on a good show. In September, the 1st, 2nd, and 4th Bombardment Wings were reorganized as the 1st, 2nd, and 3rd Air Divisions. The Third Division launched 157 B-17s accompanied by 181 from the First Division. Of the 338 total force dispatched, 262 were "effective" in reaching the target area. However, 6 September was a costly fiasco. Cloud cover over Stuttgart obscured the ball bearing factory, leaving Eighth Air Force lead bombardiers frustrated in sighting the target with their Nordens. Formations began to separate in the target search. Bombs were dropped randomly on "targets of opportunity." With aircraft now low on fuel, the attack was abandoned and headed home. Eleven ditched in the Channel due to exhausted fuel. In all, 45 B-17s were lost, 116 more damaged. A correlative cost was resentment among aircrews who knew the mission should have been recalled.

On 8 October, the 1st and 3rd Divisions (all B-17s) attacked Bremen while the 2nd Division hit Vegesack – 30 bombers lost. On the 9th more of the same: Anklam, Marienburg, Danzig and Gdynia, at a cost of 28 bombers. October 10: Munster, Coesfeld and Eschede, at a cost of 30 B-17s.

Shweinfurt Again

October 14, 1943 – aircrews of the participating groups would learn at their mission briefings that they would be re-visiting Schweinfurt. It does not stretch the imagination to sense the aircrews' reaction, knowing what happened in August. Nine groups of the 1st Division and seven of the 3rd launched 291 B-17s, of which 229 were effective in reaching the target area. Luftwaffe fighters in greater number than the August mission rose to greet them, this time with the Ju 88 lobbing rockets outside of the range of the bombers' .50 caliber machine guns with devastating effects. A rocket hit resulted in an explosion of the projectile. B-17s began taking evasive action that in turn broke up the combat box formations, leaving stragglers now easy prey for German fighters. The attack was considered more effective than the August mission, but at an unacceptable loss of 60 bombers. Seven more B-17s were lost in crashes on returning to their bases.

There was no way the Eighth could win a battle of attrition with the Luftwaffe under the engagement situation prevailing in late 1943. There was especially no way it could be won without fighter escort protection for bombers attacking targets at the extremities of their operating range. In spite of all the night and day bomber operations aimed at German war production, by the end of 1943, German factories were producing more fighters than they were losing.

In May 1943, Ira Eaker was convinced that the steady build up of Bomber Command's offensive strength and strike capability had reached the point that he was ready to undertake missions into

Germany to hit target objectives defined by the Casablanca Conference. There would be no escort fighters except P-47s, each with an external fuel tank that could barely reach the German border. Eaker's persistent mind-set was such that the bomber streams could take care of themselves with their existing armament. But the high cost of attrition experienced by unescorted missions to German industrial targets, as well as concerns about their effectiveness, began to eat away Eaker's credibility at the higher levels of the American military bureaucracy.

In fact, by November 1943 it became apparent that Eaker's days as commander of the Eighth were numbered. Carl Spaatz was pressing for massive attacks by the Eighth and Fifteenth Air Forces against Nazi oil targets with timing set to begin in the spring of 1944. Eaker was aware of Arnold's dissatisfaction with his performance and the latter's intent to replace him. Arnold had reservations about targeting priorities and the pace of the air campaign against Germany. In his view, Eaker was not sending enough bombers to get adequate tonnage on the targets. Arnold wanted a more aggressive commander, one who would expand the effort. On 6 January 1944, Eaker, the man who built the Eighth, was transferred to the Mediterranean theater, making space in London for Spaatz, head of the 15th since November 1943, to take over the U.S. Strategic Air Forces in Europe. Doolittle took over the Eighth.

In the mind of this author, there is a glaring paradox about all of this that surfaces with the issue of attrition. Spaatz and Arnold pressed Eaker for more aggressive attacks on German oil and industries, well aware of the lack of escort fighters and certainly aware of the heavy casualties on raids without them. Both men seemed more than reconciled in accepting those casualties. Equally ironic, Eaker is replaced just at the time that the P-51, the solution to the escort problem, makes its appearance in the battle environment.

James "Jimmy" Doolittle was a man of unlimited gifts, a hands-on aviator with enough creative instincts to ease nicely into a leadership role with the Eighth Air Force. In my mind, Doolittle's stature as an airman is unparalleled. His military aviation rating dates to 1918, and his service extended through many gates of aviation development. His exploits in the "locust years" are replete with examples of the creativity of which he was generously endowed. After serving as a test pilot and engineer at McCook Field, Ohio, he entered the Massachusetts Institute of Technology in 1923, earning a doctorate in Aeronautics. He conducted aircraft acceleration tests at McCook that led to his master's thesis. Doolittle's service continued at McCook where he was assigned experimental duties, with side duties as an instructor pilot to the 385th Bomb Group of the Air Corps Reserve. In 1927 he was the first to perform an outside loop, then thought to be impossible and fatal if attempted. Doolittle was a pioneer in instrument flying and flew coast to coast entirely on instruments to forecast the practicality and perfection of instrument flying as we now know it. In 1925 he won the Schneider Trophy flying a Curtis R3C-2 racer equipped with pontoons at 232 MPH, and was awarded the Mackay Trophy for that feat a year later. Doolittle won the Bendix Trophy in 1931 and the Thompson Trophy in 1932. His WW II service started with his recall just after Pearl Harbor. He was promoted to Lt Col and selected to lead the 1942 attack on Tokyo for which President Roosevelt awarded him the Medal of Honor. He jumped a grade with his promotion to Brig Gen in July 1942 when he took command of the 12th Air Force in Africa. In March 1943 he took command of the 15th Air Force as a Maj Gen, leading to his selection to command the Eighth in January 1944.

The Savior—P-51D Mustang

CHAPTER 11 GLIMMERS OF HOPE

The development of a single weapon, the North American P-51 Mustang, reversed the fortunes of the Eighth Air Force, leading not only to air superiority, but eventually air supremacy. By the middle of 1944, the Luftwaffe could still strike terror into the ranks of the Eighth's bomber crews, but they could not and would not stop them. The P-51 developed with the range to penetrate along the bomber streams to targets deep in Germany. Although initially limited in numbers, Mustang escorts entered the battle for the air in December 1943. On 6 March 1944, 100 of them were over Berlin. The significance of the emerging P-51 as an escort fighter to the outcome of the air campaign in Western Europe cannot be overemphasized. Even with escorts, 69 bombers went down over Berlin on 6 March.

Robert Lovett, U.S. Assistant Secretary of War for Air, recognized the need for escort fighters, and Hap Arnold responded to prompts from Lovett. In a memorandum, Arnold directed the development of an escort fighter that could go deep into Germany with the bombers, but oddly did not mention the P-51 Mustang already in the development mix. The USAAF air staff had little interest in what would evolve into the P-51 Mustang. A prototype was built for the RAF, the Air Staff having seen the potential of the design as a fighter-bomber. Ironically, the aircraft was designed by one Edgar Schmued, who once worked for Willy Messerschmitt. Early production models were equipped with the Allison engine and were limited in performance above 15,000 miles, since the Allison had only a single stage supercharger. The B model of the aircraft was re-equipped with the Rolls-Royce Merlin, what Walter Boyne in his book *Clash of Wings* calls "a marriage made in heaven." The RAF ordered limited numbers and used the aircraft for low level ground attacks. The Merlin dramatically changed the name of the performance game. As noted earlier, fuel capacity was augmented with the installation of an 85 gallon fuel tank behind the pilot. This, with two drop tanks under the wing on both sides gave the aircraft the range needed for escorting bombers on deep missions.

The advent of the Mustang also brought about changes in tactics on both sides. When Gen Doolittle replaced Eaker as the commander of the Eighth Air Force in January 1944, the preferred tactic was to keep the newly arriving P-51 escorts close to the bomber formations with the idea of intercepting German fighters as they rose and pressed their attacks. The Luftwaffe used the same tactic in their daylight raids on London during the Battle of Britain. The basic concept was to bring the bombers back safely to their bases. The Germans paid a high price in losses. Their Bf 109 escort fighters were short on range. Keeping them close to the bombers depleted their fuel supplies to the point that when they did engage the RAF defensive fighters they had to break off the fight early because of low fuel. Doolittle recognized that the best avenue to true air superiority was to put the emphasis on destroying German fighters. He directed Gen William Kepner, commander of the Eighth Fighter Command, to release elements of the escort force from the bomber formations to go after the Bf 109s and Fw 190s before they could assemble and follow them after they pressed their attacks. Thus the "fighter sweep" technique made its way into the tactical venue. To some degree the bombers were now decoys – perhaps bait is a better word – and flight plans would be elongated to maximize the idea of luring German fighters aloft. Fighter sweeps employed increasingly stronger P-51 and P-47 units that were sent in advance of and along the bomber routes to intercept and engage defensive fighters as they assembled and rose to the attack. In essence, the German fighters could not intercept our bomber formations without themselves being intercepted. An immediate result was the elimination of the slower German twin-engine fighters, which could dwell beyond the range of the bombers' defensive firepower and lob rockets into the formations with such devastating effects.

Big Week

The Eighth Air Force was now on a course that would lead to the gradual elimination through attrition of the German fighter defense as an effective force. Eighth Air Force bomber strikes complemented the fighter tactics by going after German fighter, synthetic rubber, and ball bearing plants. Attacks on German oil production were increasing with telling effects. Winning air superiority was now both crucial and attainable. Operation Big Week took place 19-25 February 1944. Its significance in the unfolding campaign cannot be overstated. The objective was to defeat the Luftwaffe through an all out effort before the coming invasion of France by Allied forces. For the Luftwaffe, it was the beginning of the end, although that end would take many perturbations. RAF Bomber Command and the USAAF Eighth and Fifteenth Air Force Bomber Commands would combine operations against German aircraft assembly plants, aircraft component production, and ball bearing factories. Eighth and Fifteenth Air Force bomber units flew 3,800 sorties, dropped 10,000 tons of bombs, and lost 226 heavy bombers. P-51s, now in the fray, flew 3,673 sorties, and lost 28 aircraft. Looking at those numbers now gives me a lot better insight into why I longed to be a fighter pilot. Those five days of Big Week were far more costly to the Luftwaffe; some one third of their defending fighters were lost, plus an unacceptable number of pilots. Big Week is not seen as a defined victory, but rather the ushering in of a mode of operation that would eventually overcome the Luftwaffe in the weeks leading up to D-Day.

By March 1944, the Luftwaffe, for all practical purposes, was beaten. In February and March, over 4,000 German aircraft perished, and Allied planners saw no way production could overcome losses of that magnitude. Yet it was overcome, as we shall see, under the genius of Albert Speer after D-Day. Losses in German pilots were no less devastating, and their quality was henceforth in sharp decline. Meanwhile, Eighth Air Force bombers were still taking a beating. As already noted, on 6 March 1944, 69 aircraft went down on the Eighth's first Berlin raid – even with P-51 escorts. Nonetheless, the battle of attrition was now working in our favor. Where German losses were at unacceptable levels, ours were not, and both fighter and bomber components of the Eighth Air Force continued to build strength. Ongoing fighter sweeps were now taking a heavy toll on Galland's kids. Arnold, however, held that it was in the escort role that German fighters could be brought up to fight. Considering results, Arnold had it wrong.

Eaker relieved Brig Gen Newton Longfellow as commander of Twentieth Bomber Command on 1 July 1943 and replaced him with Maj Gen Frederick Anderson. A month later Maj Gen William Kepner replaced Maj Gen Frank Hunter as head of the Eighth Fighter Command. With Doolittle commanding the Eighth in February 1944, Kepner pushed for a resurgence of fighter sweeps, where P-51s were turned loose from the bomber formations to intercept German fighters as they rushed up from land, only to meet their destruction.

Into the Unknown

CHAPTER 12   JUNE 1944, INVASION SUPPORT

D-Day, 6 June 1944

The Eighth AF Bomber Command was redirected from the strategic to tactical targets to support Overlord, the D-Day invasion. There was a lot of bitter infighting among Allied commanders over the commitment of strategic bombers to the direct support of invasion forces. The plan was to put both the Eighth Air Force and RAF Bomber Commands under the control of General Dwight Eisenhower, Supreme Commander of the Allied Forces, and interdict the battlefield in combined operations by focusing on transportation and the movement of German troops and mechanized units. The American and British air commanders, Carl Spaatz and Sir Arthur Harris, resisted, and argued that attacks on German oil would be more effective. Spaatz also felt that the attacks on oil production were the best way to bring the Luftwaffe up to fight. Eisenhower's focus was on assuring the success of the invasion. The Transportation Plan, as it was called, was adopted. Both bomber commands were put under the operational control of Eisenhower and assigned railway and other targets designed to stifle movement of German resources into the battle. The effectiveness of the target shift was hard to measure in terms of its implementation and impact in the early days of the invasion. But as the battle for France unfolded, the havoc wreaked on the French railway network by the Eighth and now the Ninth Air Force B-26s and heavily armed P-47s had taken over tactical support and was devastating to German logistic support and operational movements of the Wehrmacht.

Invasion talk was widespread well before 6 June, but on the 5th. when everyone was confined to the Lavenham air base, we knew something was about to happen. The mission briefing officially announced the invasion to come off at about 2300, with take-off at first light on 6 June. The target assigned to the 837th Squadron was a bridge on the Loire River.

The 837th was one of three B-24H squadrons committed to the 487th Bomb Group's effort for Overlord. It is possible that all four squadrons were committed to the task, since it was a maximum effort.

Following assembly in formation over England, we crossed the beachhead around 0600 at an altitude of 10,000 feet (low for us) en route to our target. The vast armada in the Channel was clearly visible, as were the hulks of numerous gliders scattered along their coastal landing zones. From about a mile inland to well beyond the target area, a solid under-cast stretched its way into France. The 837th Squadron flew to the general site of its assigned bridge, but never dropped a bomb, since the objective could not be seen. According to an old press release sent to me by a British friend in 1995, some squadrons dropped their bombs using radar equipment. This surprised me since we were instructed to bomb only if we had positive visual contact. It was standard policy to avoid indiscriminate drops anywhere in France. The 487th was not equipped with radar targeting gear at that point in time anyway. I guess I would also question the accuracy of a radar-guided drop on a target as small as a bridge, typical of tactical targets. However, it is feasible that radar drops were made on German airfields to the rear of the battle area, but not by the 487th.

In supporting the invasion forces on the beachheads, we went after anything inland that was transportation-related, in order to disrupt German troop movements. Hitler's refusal to release his Panzer units did a hell of a lot more to "interdict the battlefield" than anything we did on June 6th. Then again, a lot of Eighth Air Force groups operated under different conditions covering varied targets that day. In any case, D-Day was an easy mission for the 837th, the consummate "milk run" of my experience. That was not the case for 1st Lt Norman Gross, however, and his crew of the 838th Squadron. Theirs was the only aircraft brought down by enemy action on that day. Their B-24 was last observed descending toward the Channel surface, where it crashed. None of the crew survived, nor were their bodies recovered. According to Roger Freeman, author of *The Mighty Eighth*, it was the only aircraft lost by the Eighth Bomber Command of more than 2,000 launched on D-Day.

An incredible break for the landing forces is the fact that, except for a few token sorties, the Luftwaffe never made an appearance over the Normandy beaches. Among the serendipitous elements was the weather that offered the Luftwaffe an operating advantage.

At the time of the Allied landings, the under-cast noted earlier offered the opportunity to screen German fighter-bombers from the overwhelming Allied air support protecting the beachhead. I can attest to presence of the under-cast, having flown above it. One can only speculate as to the extent of the disruption that German fighter-bombers could have brought to the landing operation. The Luftwaffe apparently lacked the muscle to lay on such an attack – due largely to Big Week and the losses sustained, not only in that devastating week but in the weeks that followed, thanks in great part to Doolittle's emphasis on flushing out German defenders to their destruction. It was a clear signal that the Luftwaffe could and would be defeated.

CHAPTER 13   OIL, TRANSPORTATION, COMMUNICATION AND MORE

In April 1944, Eighth Air Force strategists launched a major shift in target priorities. Heretofore, priority was given to ball bearing production and aircraft plants. Based on intelligence filtering into the system via ULTRA, the code name for high level German communications, it was learned that interrupting oil production was having a significant impact on Germany's wartime efforts. It is not as though oil targets were not recognized from the beginning of the bombing campaign, in fact a committee headed by Elihu Root, former U.S. Secretary of State, placed oil number three in priority behind ball bearings and aircraft production, in recognition that oil is the lifeblood of modern warfare. Now, suddenly, American target strategists recognized that hitting synthetic oil and gas production would be more damaging to Germany in the target mix than oil alone, or in fact ball bearings and munitions factories. In April, new emphasis was given to going after oil. The Eighth Air Force led the way in the target shift in Western Europe, in parallel with the 15th Air Force campaign against German oil refineries in Ploesti, Romania.

Synthetic oil production facilities were well scattered; a small number were the producers of high-grade aviation fuel as well as motor fuel for vehicles. Such fuels were extracted from coal by water under pressure. Most of the output came from two plants at Merseburg and Politz. Merseburg was bombed repeatedly by the Eighth. The former became a sinister word for bomber crews, known by them as "Mercylessburg." Politz was completely disabled and production ended.

Merseburg may have been the synthetic oil target most feared by Eighth Bomber Command airmen, but Leurna, a plant near

Merseberg, was the most vigorously defended industrial target in Germany. Bomber Command attacks on Leurna from 12 May 1944 to 5 April 1945 took the lives of 1,280 Eighth Air Force airmen with little to show for that high price. Results were limited by the intensity of the defensive environment, both Luftwaffe fighters and flak. Heavy flak, smoke screens, and smoke from burning oil tanks limited visibility even on clear days to the point where target location for bombardiers was difficult. Even with good visibility using the Norden bombsight, it is estimated that only 29 percent of the bombs dropped fell within the confines of the production complex – using radar it was about 5 percent. In three separate attacks the Eighth lost a total of 119 bombers with little result – not one bomb fell within the Leurna complex.

I had the good fortune not to take the Merseberg tour, but did manage one or two others – Misburg and most notably Lutzkendorf that I mentioned briefly in the first paragraph of the Prologue. It was my third combat mission and, for me, graphic introduction to the combat environment I had entered. Merseburg was the place that I lost my hut mate on 25 November 1944 – casualties that day included Loye Lauraine, one of the original 837th Squadron pilots and my hut mate through my entire experience at Lavenham. While Elihu Root's advisory committee to Hap Arnold focused the ensuing bombardment effort on oil, British counterparts, operational research pioneer Solly Zuckerman and Air Chief Marshal Arthur Tedder, went for transportation. This, in the company of the oil campaign, wrought havoc in Germany largely after D-Day, when the RAF Bomber Command under Harris had some diversion from fire bombing German cities. In a sense, this shift brought Harris back to the targeting objectives set by POINTBLANK, but the bombing of German cities under Harris did not end there.

Because of D-Day, Eighth Bomber Command did not fly another strategic mission until 20 June 1944. In reviewing Freeman's *The*

Mighty Eighth, I note that there were 43 attacks on oil related targets by the end of 1944. Targets included synthetic fuel plants, oil refineries, and oil storage facilities. Sixteen of these missions included attacks on Merseburg. By now mission planning included a mix of targets from ball bearing factories, aircraft production, munitions facilities, airfields, and transportation. Attacks on transportation targets and airfields increased significantly when the Eighth Air Force and RAF Bomber Command were placed under the command of Dwight Eisenhower, especially on the heels of the invasion.

Anatomy Of A Mission

To illustrate the growing size and application of air power, I offer the following: a mission flown on 11 December 1944. The raid amassed the largest number of aircraft deployed on a single mission up to that date.

Eighth Bomber Command Attack – 11 Dec 1944			
Air Division	Deployed	Target	Tonnage
1st B-17	334	Frankfurt	918
1st B-17	182	Manheim	506
2nd B-24	353	Hanau	771
		Karlsruhe	21
2nd B-24	177	Maximilliansau	396
3rd B-17	540	Manheim	506
TOTALS 3,949		1,586	
Note: Bombers were supported by 841 P-51s and P47s			
Note: Objectives were bridges and rail targets			

May 28 was a very active day for the Eighth Bomber Command – Lutzkendorf for me was a rude awakening into the hellish world I was entering. If I live a thousand years, I will not forget that day. More than 1,300 heavies were launched to attack some 30 targets in Germany, most of them oil targets. Of the 1,300 bombers launched, about 900 were classified as "effectives," i.e., able to press their attacks with drops on targets. Thirty-two were lost.

The mission plan called for an easterly approach to a navigational fix just north of the target area. The initial point (IP) spacing was usually set to allow ten minutes or so on the bomb run to the target. Between the IP and the target area, the lead bombardiers would align their Norden sights with the target and calculate the point in space where the bombs would be dropped. From the IP our squadron executed a right turn on a southerly track in its approach to the drop point.

The next ten minutes over Lutzkendorf were filled with terror. Altitude was held constant with very minimal course corrections, which meant that over a heavily defended area we were at maximum vulnerability to flak. Even the German fighter pilots, bent as they were to get at us, did not enter those flak barrages. For this we were grateful. A signal for an impending German fighter attack over a heavily defended city was when the flak barrage abruptly ceased. In any case, the German gunners could have a field day with anyone who flew straight and level, as we would learn firsthand a few missions later.

Each of the 487th's three squadrons went in sequentially a few minutes apart from the IP. Chuck Eubank and I were leading the rear low element of three aircraft. With Eubank at the controls, I had little to do other than look as we approached the target area. The sky ahead was alive with flak bursts and the hail storm of shrapnel emanating from them. This awesome barrage meant that the German guns were bracketing an area they knew we had to fly through. During this time intercom chatter ceased.

Chuck's eyes were glued to the belly of the B–24 leading the second element – he was the consummate non-emotional man. I rarely saw him visibly angry – except for the time I overslept in Alamogordo – and he hid his fears very well. But as the formation began the right turn over the IP to enter the bomb run, Chuck froze for a second or two. Fascinated by the flak, he was looking straight ahead at the barrage as the aircraft in front of us slid away to the right. Instinctively, I nudged the control column ever so lightly to end his distraction. This simple act on my part was for me another moment of truth. Like those men in Pickett's charge, I knew that I would have to face the carnage with the others. I had no choice. Additionally, it was the first time I would really assert myself and make a positive contribution to our mission performance. The business on the practice mission where Chuck and I fought for control of the aircraft was purely an instinctive reaction for survival.

Our turn was slightly late as a result of that moment of hesitation, and the rest of the squadron was well in front of our element when we turned on course toward the target. We caught up on the bomb run, and the flak caught up with us. We were most vulnerable from the IP to the drop point. Evasive turns and altitude changes on the bomb run were taboo, and only small corrections in heading were made as the lead bombardier picked up the target and tracked it with the optics of his Norden.

Think of a cube-like structure several thousand feet deep suspended over a large metropolitan area filled with thousands of pulsating black bursts, and at the heart of each burst a mean orange core. "Christ, we're going to have to fly through THAT!" I thought. All I could do was sit here and watch. Our navigator Frank Nelson in his piece published in *One Last Look* was a bit cavalier about the flak and getting the job done, but I will confess that I was awed – "scared shitless," as we were wont to say in the lexicon of the Eighth Air Force in 1944. I experienced this scene many times after Hanover, and it never got any easier. I used to try to think of my body as a small ball tucked away safely under a flak helmet where I would not be hit, but there was no escape from the reality of the flak. At Hanover I didn't even have a flak helmet – they hadn't been issued yet. We were ten souls trapped in our suspended aluminum cage in a hailstorm of deadly steel chards with nowhere to go and no way to run.

I am always amused when I see World War II films depicting aircraft in flak barrages. The pilot figure, usually wearing his crushed hat over which the earphones draped Hollywood style, struggles with the controls as the aircraft bucks like an incensed rodeo bronco. Sounds of bursting shells fill the soundtrack. In my romance with flak I never heard more than a barely audible thud or felt more than a sensation like a mild bump from the concussion of near misses. In the real world of air combat there were none of the special effects of filmdom. Flak bursts were essentially silent but nonetheless a thoroughly sinister visual menace from which there was no exit, except perhaps a direct hit. What I do remember are the sounds of flak shards hitting the aircraft. When such debris entered the bomb bay and rattled around against those 500- and 1,000-pound bomb casings, the results produced crisp "pings" easily heard above the normal din inside an aircraft. That sound always got my undivided attention, especially when I knew the bombs were armed. "Holy shit," I would say to myself as I purged the unthinkable from my mind. I tried to deal with the flak by not looking at it (though we all would later recover scraps of flak as souvenirs). I welcomed my stint at the controls, since my eyes never left the wing tip or tail turret of the aircraft on which we kept our position in the formation. Even then, there wasn't much solace, since the other aircraft was usually framed in flak bursts anyway.

As we approached the target, I witnessed for the first time a B–24 going down in flames. It came from above and passed to our right about a hundred yards or so in a straight out dive. Its fuselage aft of the trailing edge of the wing and empennage were completely gone – probably from a direct flak hit. The fire emanated from the oxygen tanks stowed just above the center wing box in what was left of the aft fuselage. It burned bright white as opposed to the yellowish-orange color associated with fuel fires. I was transfixed by the sight and can see it clearly to this day – over half a century later. That tail-less B-24 went by and then pulled up in a sharp climb. After its speed bled away, that great wing B-24 wing stalled and the aircraft tumbled end over end like a falling leaf, soon entering another dive, followed by another stall, and so on. That tumbling leaf sequence continued all the way down until it passed from my sight far below. I saw no parachutes; it required little imagination to realize the fate of that crew. The waist section took the hit, and the gunners in that section could hardly have survived the blast and shrapnel. Gravitational forces in that wildly gyrating aircraft in its death throes literally pinned those on the flight deck and in the nose in their seats. In the book *The Air War in Europe*, there is a photograph of a B–24 going straight down without its tail. The caption says the aircraft went down over "Northern Germany in 1944." It could well be a photo of the event I witnessed – I'll never know.

After bombs away in circumstances like Lutzkendorf, the squadron would exit the bomb run in a turning descent or climb. For me it was the exit from the flak. Remembering again *Catch 22*, Yossarian would sit there in the nose of his B-25 saying after the bomb drop "turn, TURN, for Christ's sake, TURN." It has never been portrayed more aptly, because that is exactly what went through my head every time, and anybody else's head that contained an iota of the survival instinct.

We recovered at Lavenham on 28 May without incident. Eubank

and the rest of us exited the aircraft thankful for the gift of survival. The prevailing mood was one of relief. We made our way directly to the operations building where we shed and stowed our gear. During that process, the Red Cross girls were on deck in their mobile snack bar to greet us with coffee, sandwiches, and doughnuts. This nourishment was badly needed to supplement the candy bars we had eaten in the air after removing our oxygen masks during the descent from bombing altitude. Also on deck were the medics with the post-mission whiskey – Johnny Walker scotch, if we got lucky. I quickly learned that one shot of whatever it was in an already exhausted body after long hours in a pressure cooker was enough to render one nearly unconscious. Of course, there were the cigarettes, handed out free in little packs of three.

All this was considered to be very good for our morale. Well, the Red Cross girls were. I regard these girls among the unsung heroines of WW II. They, like the female ferry pilots of our American WASPs, have never been accorded the recognition they deserve for their contributions to the war effort. What the Red Cross girls did for us airmen pales in comparison to the uplifting support they provided our ground forces on the beaches of Normandy and later as the invasion swept through Europe.

Next came the mission debriefing where the aircrews were assembled at tables and interrogated by the group intelligence officers. Probing questions always focused on target observations, flak and fighter opposition where encountered, claims of fighter kills, weather, and, most important, bombing results. Answering questions about strike patterns was the purview of the bombardier who had the best seat in the house. It was he who filled out the strike forms. Over the course of my missions I could see columns of black smoke rising from target areas struck by units ahead of ours. I never once saw the bombs from my squadron hit anything – even the ground.

While the bombardier usually witnessed the explosive flashes and smoke from his bombs as they landed in the target area, he was not in a position to accurately assess damage. Strike damage assessments were accomplished after mission debriefing by photo interpretation teams using imagery provided by the strike cameras carried in the aircraft. Follow up post-mission reconnaissance flights provided the true measure of bombing results. Even then, there was much conjecture about results.

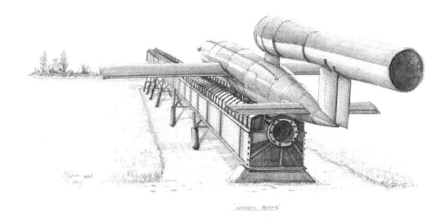

London Bound

161

CHAPTER 14   LONDON AND THE V-1

Hitler's promise of secret weapons and his quest for an effective bombing capability would prove to be no idle threat. At the German weapons development center in Peenemunde, his scientists and engineers were making good progress on several new jet aircraft and unmanned weapons of destruction. Two of the latter were operational by the spring of 1944, and Hitler ordered their use as weapons of vengeance against England's civilian population. Their very limited performance hardly put them in a position to achieve pinpoint bombing accuracies.

Designed by Satan himself, the V-1 was an ungainly pilotless contraption, half bomb, and half airplane – the first of the cruise missile genre. It was in a compact package 27 feet in length with a span of 18 feet, and it weighed 4,900 pounds. The aircraft manufacturer, Gerhard Fiesler Werk, made the airframe. The engine was an Argus manufactured pulsejet, essentially a ramjet with a pulsed ignition action. Launched by rocket from a catapult, engine ignition began when it reached 224 mph. The V-1 cruised at a speed of 360 mph and was guided by a magnetic compass and a gyro flight control system that kept it stable in flight and guided it along a pre-set course to the "target" area. Engine ignition was cut at a pre-set time, at which point the V-1 simply stalled and nosed over (the V-1 did not glide) in a vertical dive to the impact point. The V-1 carried a payload of about 1,800 pounds.

These weapons were first used against London on 13 June 1944. During that summer, 2,000 V-1s were dispatched against England from their launch sites in France and Belgium, killing 6,000 people and wounding 40,000 others. Dubbed "Buzz Bombs" by the British, the flight of the V-1 was very visible as well as audible, and RAF Spitfire pilots became adept at intercepting and destroying many before they reached their targets. Their technique was innovative – approaching from above and behind, the Spitfire would accelerate with enough speed to overtake the V-1. When abreast at a matching speed, the Spitfire pilot would slip a wing tip under the wing tip of the V-1 and apply a lifting force with the aileron to roll the V-1 enough to upset its autopilot's gyro. The V-1 would go vertical to its destruction, hopefully in an open field.

My second and third trips to London were far more interesting than that night I spent in the train station with a demanding female! While none of the Eubank crew had even heard of them, I would learn about the V-1 first hand from the bombee rather than bomber point of view. The first episode was most likely between 24-30 June 1944, where a six-day hiatus in my mission activities is shown in my flight records.

In that June week of 1944, Eubank, Nelson, Wilcox, and I went to London without a room reservation or anything. We just showed up, as was our custom. We tried for billets at the Cumberland and one or two other hotels of note without success. One of the hotel desk clerks that had to turn us away suggested we try Brown's Hotel, leaving a somewhat spurious notion in our heads about the place. So to Browns we went – the four of us. It was a very pleasant surprise as far as the accommodations were concerned. However, there were some very staid and proper English retired people in residence. Looking somewhat askance down their noses as they regarded us, they were taken back by this invasion of rather crude Yanks. I think we were about as welcome as the American cockroach.

London at night during the war was a city of shadows – cars moving about with headlights and taillights cowled in metal shrouds so that only red and white slits could be seen at street level, but not by the invading enemy above. When eyes adjusted to the shadowy darkness, vehicles were nothing more than moving shadows with their slits of light. The other moving shadows were people. Lighting inside the pubs, hotels, businesses, and homes was very subdued. Windows were heavily draped to prevent the escape of a single ray of light. Strict air raid wardens patrolled everywhere to make sure no shafts of light radiated from windows and doors. Such were the air raid precautions of a people heavily bombed by the Germans. When the shadows vanished with the light of day, air raid damage could be seen everywhere.

So it was this night at Browns. Eubank and I shared a room. There was a bath (sheer luxury), twin beds separated by a night table, and a pair of heavily shrouded windows draped in some kind of deep red velvet. Chuck and I turned in at the same time that night. We had found little to do. Chuck was married, and he was absolutely incorruptible in his faithfulness to his wife Mildred. I never saw him step outside of that relationship in the time I knew him. Frank Nelson was the same way. Wilcox and I were the hell raisers.

We had just turned out the light and were lying in those beds in total darkness when I heard the distinct Doppler sound effect produced by an approaching aircraft. I knew it to be an aircraft of some sort, but the engine noise was different — something like an in-line engine with a slow, but loud, beat. The growling, throbbing, pulsating noise grew ever louder as it approached the heart of London.

Then for about thirty seconds there was total silence — nothing except the street noises below our window — followed by the damndest explosion I have ever heard. It was close. Everything rattled and danced in the room. The windowpanes shook but somehow held. I turned on the lamp between our beds. Chuck and I both shot bolt upright and stared at each other. What the hell was that?

German raids by night on London with intruder aircraft were common, but they had long since given up on the massed air attacks. Chuck and I concluded that we had witnessed a night intruder raid by a single German aircraft, doused the light, and went to sleep. The next morning we learned about the V-1s.

Going back to Brown's Hotel in 1988 was like going back to Lavenham; I had to do it. Like almost everything else, it looked smaller than my mind's eye had it, but it was the same right down to its stuffiness. If I had been taken inside blindfolded, I would have known where I was. Brown's, incidentally, is now a world-class facility.

On another visit to London some time after the Brown's Hotel episode, I was walking along a crowded Oxford Street late at night near the Cumberland Hotel, which sits directly across the street from Hyde Park. The Cumberland occupied the whole block. Two streets that run off Oxford flank the ends of the hotel.

The night was smog-laden, as usual, and pitch-black – the familiar floating slits of red and white light from moving vehicles and the shadowy forms of many people and buildings were silhouetted in the London mist.

Off in the distance my ear picked up the same unmistakable sound I had heard that night at Brown's – the pulsating roar of a ramjet approaching out of the darkness. Directly overhead the engine stopped. There was instant bedlam; people started running in all directions. I could not see much, but the pounding of feet sounded like a cattle stampede. Off we ran. I was running like everyone else – running like hell with no idea of where I was going. Suddenly I was swept into a staircase leading underground to a side entrance of the Cumberland as the explosion erupted with the attendant tremors. The warhead of that V-1 struck just on the other side of Hyde Park. The entire episode lasted but a few minutes.

CHAPTER 15   JULY 1944: FLAK BAIT

8 July 1944

July 8 was another busy day for the Eighth Bomber Command. Over a thousand bombers rose from their East Anglican bases and set out against enemy airfields and transportation hubs in France, Belgium and the Netherlands. Strikes against German occupied airfields were never that easy, but we were hopeful for a "milk run." It would prove to be anything but.

Eighth Air Force bombers and their fighter escorts took off from places with colorful English names, such as Bury St. Edmunds, Sudbury, Molesworth, Thorpe-Abbotts, Duxford, Martlesham Heath, and so on. Over a hundred American air bases dotted an area of about 11,000 English square miles. A piece of real estate that size would be swallowed by a couple of fair sized counties in my state of Virginia. The analogy often used – and I can't think of a better one – is that at least one hundred air fields were packed into this small area of real estate like scores of planes would be in a single naval aircraft carrier.

Of the thousand plus bombers launched on 8 July, less than half made actual target runs, due mostly to poor weather in the target areas. However, weather over England was clear, as were the Channel and French coast.

The 487th launched two squadrons led by Capt Larry Herman, 837th Squadron operations officer. Both squadron formations comprised twelve B-24Hs. We were leading the low rear element of three aircraft. That put us in the slot with one aircraft on each wing. Eubank and I would fly formation in this position in our usual 20-minute stints, with eyes riveted on the tail gun turret of the aircraft above and in front of us.

The squadron was approaching the Belgian coast at 16,000 feet climbing to our bomb run altitude, which was in the 20-22,000 foot range. The aircraft was heavy with fuel and the maximum bomb load at take off from our base at Lavenham.

We were hit by flak with absolutely no reason to think we were doing anything more than entering enemy territory at a usually docile point, but the flak nailed us. There were no telltale flak bursts ahead to warn us. Penetration of enemy territory was made along the English Channel coast between Ostend and Dunkirk near the border of France and Belgium. It was a corridor selected by our intelligence people as the best bet for flak-free entry. German flak concentrations were carefully mapped based on intelligence reports and their locations were given to Eighth Air Force aircrews at the pre-mission briefings. Flight paths to target areas were plotted with the idea of avoiding the hot spots. But the Germans were not at all stupid. They moved the flak guns (88mm field pieces) around on barges and rail facilities when they picked up our routines. The Germans positioned a flak battery in the Ostend-Dunkirk corridor on 8 July. They were tracking our formation and calculating the firing equation, as opposed to their alternative flak defense, which was a barrage, set very visibly in our paths. Thus, there was no warning. There were probably half a dozen guns and only one salvo, but one had our number. Whatever got us went off just below, concentrating under the left wing, knocking out both engines on the port side. We were lucky at that, perhaps a microsecond from a direct hit.

The initial indication of a problem was a sharp yaw of the aircraft's nose to the left. Chuck responded immediately with aileron and rudder inputs in an attempt to arrest the swing to the left and dumped the nose to maintain airspeed. We were quickly out of the formation.

Chuck was on the intercom simultaneously. Pilot to crew, "We've been hit."

My eyes instinctively scanned the engine instruments. The number one tachometer needle was winding its way up the dial toward the red line for maximum rpm. I ripped off my oxygen mask and yelled to Chuck, "Number one is a runaway, and it looks like we've lost number two."

To understand our plight, I need to explain a few things about aircraft performance in engine out situations. The B-24 would fly well on three engines and could hold altitude with two, providing the propellers on the dead engines could be "feathered." Maintaining position in formation on three engines at the higher operating altitudes (20,000 feet), however, was not possible.

The B-24's Pratt and Whitney engines were equipped with Hamilton Standard constant speed propellers. Propeller pitch was controlled with hydraulics, in turn controlled by electrical switches on the throttle quadrant in the cockpit. The propeller design incorporated the "full feathering" feature, meaning that the three blades could be rotated parallel to the thrust vector in order to stop rotation and reduce drag, should the engine fail. In normal operation, a propeller governor controlled the maximum rotation speed. If the governor failed as well as the engine, the result was usually a runaway propeller and extreme drag on the dead engine side. In engine failure situations, the aircraft will turn toward the dead engine.

Harry Ferris responded immediately to the aircraft's loss of control and was out of the top turret in a flash. Both he and Chuck removed their oxygen masks so they could communicate without depending on the intercom.

"Barney, you've got control of the aircraft; try to kill the spiral and get us over the Channel," yelled Chuck. "I've got to get number one under control."

169

Chuck ordered Ferris to feather the number two engine as he reached for the feathering button on number one. Ferris closed both the number one and two throttles, cut off fuel flow and turned off the ignition switches to both engines to offset the possibility of fire. Cutting the fuel flow to the damaged engines probably saved our butts. The number two engine responded to the feathering command, and the propeller wound down and halted as the blades reached the full-feathered position, perpendicular to the relative wind. But the tachometer needle for number one was out of sight, and the propeller refused to respond to the feathering command. The rotation of the windmilling propeller increased further as our indicated airspeed increased in the initial descent.

Chuck was now holding the feathering button in the engaged position. Turning in frustration to Ferris, "Harry, I should be able to control the runaway by holding the button in. What the hell is going on? Check the operating handbook and see if you can come up with something." He continued, "Also check the circuit breaker panel to see if we have popped one on the feathering circuit."

As I labored with the controls, Eubank and Ferris leafed through the B-24 operating handbook in efforts to get number one feathered. No one panicked; we were all too busy. But we were still going down.

"Pilot to waist," said Chuck. "Anybody back there see anything? Do we have any fire in number one and two engines? Are we losing fuel?"

"Pilot from ball turret," Pancoast responded from his position, "looks like several bursts of flak went off right under us."

"All right," Chuck replied. "Better come up out of that ball, we're going down pretty fast."

"We are trailing smoke from both one and two," Irving reported in from the left waist gun, "but I don't see any indication of fire or fuel leaks."

While Chuck and Harry struggled with number one engine, the lot fell to me to try to control the aircraft. The uncontrollable yaw and resulting descending left turn reversed our course toward the English coast and brought us over the Strait of Dover, the narrows between the French and English coasts. The Strait connects the English Channel with the North Sea. The first priority was to kill the spiral. Full right rudder with the control wheel all the way clockwise to its limit were not enough, and the spiral continued as did the descent, which we never did fully arrest. Directional control of the aircraft would prove difficult but attainable. I reduced power to the number three and four engines on the right side to stop the left turn and pulled the nose up to slow the aircraft to just above stall speed in an effort to reduce the rpm on the runaway propeller. It still took a lot of aileron input and full right rudder to keep the left wing level enough to kill the turn. There was no way I could stop the descent. Trim tabs were helpful in easing control inputs, but insufficient. I can remember my right leg jammed forward on the right rudder pedal for so long that it began to tremble. Both Chuck and I were on that rudder.

With the English coast in sight, the question now was whether we could flatten the descent enough to reach it. The runaway number one propeller's rpm was well above the red line (2,750) to 3,500, the extent of the dial's calibration. Eubank kept punching the feathering button for number one without success. Ferris checked out the circuit breaker panel and found no indication of an electrical problem. Both kept drawing blanks.

In retrospect, it is amazing to me that calmness and common sense prevailed. Chuck got back on the intercom:

171

"Pilot to bombardier."

"Go ahead, Chuck."

"Jettison the bombs, Dave."

"Roger, as soon as I open the bomb bay doors they'll be gone. They're still unarmed."

"Okay Dave, leave the bomb bay doors open after they are gone. We may have to use that exit. You guys better clear the nose now. I don't know where we're going to put this damn thing."

"Pilot to crew. We're in deep shit. Both engines on the left side are out, and we can't get control of the number one propeller. The drag from that runaway is like opening a barn door on the left side. I can see the English coastline, but there is no guarantee that we can reach it. We have the option of bailing out or ditching. If you decide to bail out, you better go now. I don't plan to ditch if I can help it. Let me know what you want to do." I signaled Chuck that I would stick with the aircraft.

Not one of the crew opted to bail out over the Channel. We never seriously considered bailing out, but a water "ditching" was very much in the offing. The prospects of surviving a water landing in a parachute were poor at best. The prospects of ditching were not much better. Unlike the B-17, a good ditching aircraft with its low wing, the B-24 had a high wing, which meant that the fuselage took the brunt of the impact. It usually broke just forward of the wing's leading edge, and the nose would dig into and under the water's surface, tough on those crewmen on the flight deck – me, for example.

Wilcox salvoed the bomb load minutes later and we decided to close the bomb bay doors in case we had to ditch. There was a perceptible response from the aircraft to the lightened load, but number one propeller was winding away. The descent continued as we passed through 7,000 feet.

With the 8,000 pound bomb load now gone, we turned our attention to reducing the rate of descent as much as we could by raising the nose and increasing power on the good engines to manage a safe airspeed with directional control. The objective now was a rate of descent we thought would get us back over land, at the same time maintaining a speed just above the stall threshold. This was also necessary to try to reduce the rotational speed of the number one propeller – the slower the airspeed, the slower the propeller rpm and therefore reduced drag. At this juncture we tried something really stupid. Ferris got back into the upper turret and brought his twin 50s to bear on that propeller and opened fire. Lucky for us, he never hit anything. Had he done so we probably would have lost a blade or a good chunk of one that could have shaken the aircraft apart. Thankfully, Ferris aborted the effort after failing to get a hit.

Eubank was now flying the aircraft, having abandoned efforts to shut down the number one propeller. We had traded a lot of altitude to maintain a safe airspeed with the good engines throttled back some during the descent, but eventually had to trade some airspeed to hold altitude. When we crossed the English coast we were 500 feet above sea level now at minimum control speed with full power on the good engines trying to stay airborne long enough to find someplace to put the aircraft on the ground. We crossed near Clacton-on-Sea, which lay on a straight-line course from where we were hit over the Belgian coast at Ostend to our airfield at Lavenham.

I leaned across the cockpit, "Chuck, I've got a runway in sight, dead ahead and on our course." Luck of the Irish, serendipity or whatever, it was as though God in his great mercy had just planted that runway there to catch us.

"Roger, I see it. Let's go for it. It's that or a ploughed field if we can stay airborne long enough to find one."

We landed straight in on that runway. It turned out to be RAF base Bradwell Bay, at the time an operating base for de Havilland Mosquitos. With no radio contact, Ferris fired red flares to alert the ground crews to our approach. Both landing gear struts were fully extended and locked when we touched down. The third engine failed from overwork on the approach before touchdown, but we had the runway "made" and held the gear extension to the last second to make sure. There was enough momentum through the landing roll to clear the runway. We were very lucky – never even had to make an approach turn to that runway. It's really not surprising – in 1944, airfields were everywhere in England, especially in the eastern portion along the coast where we landed. The entire episode took about thirty minutes. Eubank did a superb job of judging that landing. When I reflect on how he put us in hub-deep mud in one of Mr. Alston's fields just two months earlier, I marvel at how he saved us with the landing of his life when the chips were down.

I remember the RAF people at the scene regarding that B-24 with considerable interest. We were all out of the aircraft inspecting the damage. The number one propeller rotated easily when pushed gently by hand; there was zero compression. The engine had disintegrated internally. I reached into the supercharger waste gate just behind the turbine and removed a hand full of debris having the consistency of ground beef. There was a gaping hole in the leading edge of the wing between numbers one and two engine. Obviously we did not know it at the time, but there was no way we could have feathered that number one propeller. The flak had shredded the leading edge of the left wing between numbers one and two engines, taking out not only both engines, but also destroying all the wiring – including the feathering circuit to number one, which was channeled through that area. The aircraft

174

was totaled and never flew again.

We made the return trip to Lavenham in the back end of an army truck. The crew's mood on return seemed suppressed by the experience. Within an hour we had gone through an unbelievable airborne event, and there were the ten of us bumping along in the back of a truck. The reality of what we had been through began to sink in, and we all became lost in our thoughts. For me, the "next mission" syndrome began to creep into my head. What if – ?

Overall, nine aircraft were lost by the Eighth Bomber Command over the continent, and seven more including our B-24 were written off with battle damage. Herman's B-24 was hit in the same barrage that got us, and he had to abort the mission as well. Post mission records indicate that those aircraft of the 487th that did make it to the target area made a successful strike.

My 19th mission marked the end of the line for B-24H aircraft SN 42-52748. On 14 July, I would fly mission number 20 in a brand new B-24H assigned as our replacement aircraft. I would go on to fly three more missions in that replacement B-24H. Unlike its camouflaged predecessor, it was unpainted. Paint added surprisingly to aircraft weight and drag as well. Our Eighth Air Force leaders came to the conclusion that camouflage paint schemes did very little to obscure us from German radar and wisely did away with it. The new aircraft was different in other ways. Gone were the steel slabs behind our seats and on the outside cockpit area surfaces, and the bullet proof glass was gone as well. Instead, the pilot and copilot seats were shrouded in a steel structure that resembled an open coffin in which the seats nestled. Otherwise it was a just another B-24H performing no differently and certainly no better than the others I flew – paint or no paint.

B-17G

Photo Courtesy USAF Archive

CHAPTER 16   CONVERSION
TO THE B-17

Converting to the B-17G brought some mixed feelings. Having never even set foot in a B-17, I knew the aircraft would be a better performer than the B-24H, especially in terms of formation flying at high altitude. On the negative side, I also knew mission target selections would be tough involving penetrations deep into Germany and very active German fighter opposition.

The training we received was minimal – neither thorough nor very intensive. A B-17 mobile training unit was brought to the base to conduct classes covering the aircraft's characteristics, engines, mechanical and electronic systems and armament. From a pilot's standpoint, I suppose the exposure was adequate, but I would hardly describe it as satisfying the demand for more intimate familiarity about what made things tick. Learning about the aircraft was coupled with flight training for the pilots and flight engineers. We shot a bunch of touch and go landings and flew some formation. I took to the B-17 immediately. Although the 487th was withdrawn from combat operations during the two-week training period, two of our aircraft were lost in a mid-air collision of a B-17 and B-24 over the Lavenham airfield.

The reasons for the conversion of B-24 groups to the B-17 warrant some consideration. The Third Air Division of the Eighth Bomber Command evolved as a mix of B-17 and B-24 groups commanded in the first half of 1944 by Curtis LeMay. I have often wondered about target assignments for our B-17 groups compared to those of the Second Air Division of which all groups were equipped with the B-24. I have concluded that aircraft performance was a key factor in target assignments. In any event, LeMay used his B-17 force for the longer range, more difficult targets in Germany. One strong factor had to do with standardizing equipment to minimize the logistics problems that came with providing support for two aircraft types. When he had to decide which aircraft it would be, he opted for the B-17's better overall performance in combat. Two factors dominantly drove that decision: altitude and formation flying.

Comparing the two aircraft based on my own flight experience, I concluded that the B-17 was by far the better aircraft in the European combat arena. It is true that the B-24 nominally had more range at 10,000 feet, was about 10 mph faster (indicated air speed), and had a larger bomb bay than the B-17, although the gross weights and payloads were about the same. The B-24 struggled at 20,000 feet and above and was difficult to fly in formation with higher fuel consumption. B-17s went after their targets at 26,000-28,000 feet, which gave them higher true airspeeds and equal range with that edge in speed, to say nothing of being at a better altitude for contending with enemy flak.

Indicated airspeed is what a pilot reads on the instrument panel indicator. Aircraft speed is measured with an impact device called a Pitot tube. As altitude increases, air density decreases, thus distorting the actual velocity at which the aircraft is traveling. In other words, the aircraft must move farther to pass through the same number of molecules of air at higher altitude to exert the same amount of pressure on the orifice of the Pitot tube. Thus the aircraft at high altitude is always moving faster than the airspeed instrument indicates. Correcting the indicated airspeed for the lighter air density yields what is called true airspeed. The B-24 cruised at 160 mph indicated airspeed compared to 150 mph for the B-17. These were nominal operating cruise speeds for the two aircraft in combat operations, selected to optimize fuel management (There was no reason why a B-17 could not cruise at 160 MPH indicated air speed). But in terms of true airspeed the B-17 was actually faster because it flew higher. For example, the true airspeed of a B-24 at 20,000 feet was 215 mph, but was 235 mph for the B-17 at 28,000 feet. I calculated these numbers by using the indicated air speeds (160 mph and 150 mph respectively) and applied -35 and -45 degrees centigrade, respectively, for the two altitudes, i.e., 20,000 feet (B-24) and 28,000 (B-17). Actual true airspeed calculations would, obviously, depend on actual density altitudes and measured temperatures at those altitudes. No consideration is made for winds aloft (they would generally be stronger at the higher altitude) because the routes to the target and the reverse courses from it would yield a no wind factor at either altitude.

The B-24 never performed up to its billing. The aircraft design incorporated a high aspect ratio wing (wide span, narrow chord) with the "Davis" airfoil-shaped elliptically, both on the upper and lower surfaces. The conventional wing design of that period used airfoil shapes that were more or less flat on the bottom side with a much wider chord. The four 1200 horse powered Pratt and Whitney R1830 engines were turbo supercharged for high altitude performance. While the engines could deliver, the wing design apparently did not. The result was an operating altitude lower than optimum for the European theater of operation, about 18,000-22,000 feet, and a trucky feel in the control responses for the pilots at those altitudes. When at the controls, I always felt the B-24 was "mushing" along in a nose-high attitude just "hanging on the props," as we used to say. To maintain level flight in formation, engine power settings had to be kept high for long periods. Engine rpm ranged from 2,300-2,500 under those conditions. Even at much lower altitudes, in the 8,000-10,000 foot range, I always found the nose of the B-24 hunting around like a hyper dog in search of a hydrant, requiring constant aileron, elevator, and rudder corrections to maintain course and a level attitude. The aircraft simply lacked that stable "hands off" feeling that pilots love when control pressures are removed with the trim tabs. By comparison,

179

the missions I flew in the B-17 were at 26,000-28,000 feet. Control inputs were soft and the response instant and firm. The aircraft felt as stable at high altitude as it did at those medium altitude ranges. The B-17 was far easier to fly in formation.

Over the years since the war, there have been endless debates comparing the performance of these two aircraft. B-24 veterans will heatedly defend the character of their aircraft, and I am sure many would question my conclusions. In fairness to the B-24, our aircraft went through a modification program when we arrived in the UK that added considerable weight. Many things were added, such as bulletproof glass around the cockpit and slabs of steel to protect the pilots. Yet we operated within the established weight envelope. With me, the bottom line in my bias for the B-17 can be summed up in a word: performance. Perhaps the best way to characterize performance differences in the two aircraft is to look at the target assignments. The B-17 units of the Third Division were getting all the deep targets in Germany and on the fringes of their range elsewhere, while the B-24 groups were getting targets in France and Belgium mostly in support of the ground forces after D-Day. Target assignments of the 487th certainly followed this pattern both before and after the conversion from the B-24 to the B-17.

As July drew to a close, the Eubank Crew was assigned a spanking new B-17G, serial number 43-46307. It was a clear skin beauty with yellow wing tips, tail surfaces and a chevron design on the right wing. One leg of the chevron was yellow, the other red.

CHAPTER 17   AUGUST 1944:
TARGET GERMANY

It was another month signaling changes in the combat scene, both in terms of target strategy and tactical mutations. When Eisenhower released the Eighth Bomber Command from its role in tactical support of the invasion, strikes aimed at strategic target objectives were resumed on 20 June 1944. However, a mix of the two objectives would follow in the months ahead. Missions aimed at interdicting the battlefield continued. From 20 June through the end of the month, there were 22 bombing missions of which all but four went after tactical targets. In July, of 24 missions flown, the mix was 13 tactical, 11 strategic, and in August, of 24 missions flown the mix was even. Tactical support would continue as Allied ground forces moved inexorably toward the Rhine River. Missions to targets in Germany focused on oil and transportation. Tactical missions tended to follow the army's march toward Berlin. This pattern would continue through the end of the war with the distinction fading as the end approached. To illustrate: bombing a marshaling yard or major rail terminal in a city was complemented by USAAF fighter bombers attacking anything and everything that moved on rails, roads, rivers, and bridges.

As advised by our intelligence people, August would also see the products of German innovation: the Me 262 and Me 163 were now visible above our formations. Of the two, the Me 262 had the potential to limit the flow of Eighth Air Force bombers in Germany, but while the capability was demonstrated, its potential was never reached.

The Messerschmitt 262 went into production in early 1944 after a development period marked by technical problems in performance. The aircraft was equipped with two Jumo 004 turbojet engines.

Armament included four Mk 108 30 mm cannons and two-dozen 55 mm R4M rockets. Early deliveries were slow with 28 in June 1944, 59 in July, and 20 in August. A total of 1,430 were built in dispersed facilities – low profile structures and forest clearings, another testament to German innovation. Flight characteristics of the aircraft had good and bad aspects. Acceleration was slow, dangerously slow on take off, and in an attack mode, it was difficult to reduce overtaking speed when in a firing situation to allow time for aiming – there were no speed brakes. The Me 262 was no dog fighter; its great asset was its speed that could not be matched by our fighters. In the attack mode, from well above the bomber formation, it could enter a shallow dive and easily fly through the fighter screen at high speed to "bounce" its target and then easily outrace anything that followed.

On 1 August, my first mission in the new B-17G was against the German airfield at Tours, France. We were one of 1,300 bombers sent against German airfields in France and transportation-related targets in support of the ground forces. It was a welcome target for me, since I assumed all my B-17 missions would probably be flown against targets deep in Germany. The mission was uneventful for us and relatively so for the rest of the Eighth Air Force strike force. Only five aircraft were lost.

The downside of the conversion to the B-17 was that the targets would now be much more vigorously defended, in terms of duration and expected opposition. This lends credence to the fact that the B-17s were being used by Eighth Air Force operations directors at longer ranges than the B-24. Again, performance was the driving factor. For me, three of my eleven B-17 missions were against targets in France. Eight were against strategic targets in Germany.

The chain of tough targets I would experience for the remainder of my tour began on 5 August when the 487th was dispatched to

Magdeburg. It was a crystal clear day with a routine visual assembly and flow into the bomber stream, which numbered more than 1,000 aircraft. In the morning briefing we were advised by our intelligence officer that we might now begin to see German rocket and jet-powered aircraft, but in very limited numbers. Overall, conventional German fighter concentrations were expected to be active.

By this juncture in the air war, the Allies had achieved complete air superiority. As we have seen, the Eighth Bomber Command gained the air advantage over the Luftwaffe with the introduction early in 1944 of the long range P-51 escort fighter. By August, the Luftwaffe was overwhelmed with American power in the daytime and Britain's at night. There would be no let up. German fighter defenses weakened as production was disrupted and oil supplies became scarce, but worst of all, they were running out of manpower. By now, flak was our worst enemy. A maximum Luftwaffe fighter defense effort would at this point be about 500 aircraft to counter at least that many of our fighters and the 1,000 aircraft bomber stream. German fighters could gang up on a few groups wreaking their usual havoc, but they could not stop us.

Thus it was on 5 August. In the clear skies over Germany, the awesome power of the Eighth Bomber Command became apparent to me for the first time from the airborne perspective. It was like a vast aerial parade with groups all in line. The long line split into forks as it approached the German border. Several groups ahead of our formation were visible by the sun glint from their natural aluminum skinned aircraft. I remember the scene so vividly – hundreds of sun specks in the cloudless blue sky. Crisscrossing white contrails above our 26,000-foot altitude suggested the presence of our escorts, but they were nowhere to be seen. Constraints shackling escort fighters to the bombers had been removed, and our P-51s were now intercepting German fighters as they rose to the battle scene. The results proved to be exactly what General Doolittle wanted: lure the German fighters aloft with our bombers to their ultimate destruction by American fighters.

The group in front of ours came under heavy attack by German fighters that had penetrated our escort screen. From my distant perch to the rear of that unfortunate unit, German fighters seemed like a pack of hungry wolves circling their prey, little black specks in queues on either flank of the sparkling points of reflected sunlight, waiting to make their firing passes. There were no U.S. fighters visible at this point. A column of smoke from a dying B-17 trailed earthward. Our group continued on unchallenged, but my attention was soon diverted to another matter.

Our intelligence briefing that morning proved to be correct. Well above the snaking vapor trails of our fighters were more contrails, much higher and in an orbital pattern. These emanated from rocket powered Messerschmitt 163s and Messerschmitt turbo-jet powered 262s. The Me 163 as a fighter species evolved from German technology advances at Peenemunde, but it would pose no serious threat because of limited numbers and even more limited performance. The aircraft took off under its own rocket power, dropped its landing gear and climbed rapidly to high altitude under power. The engine shut down when the limited fuel supply was exhausted. The 163 made one diving pass with no power. Following the single firing pass, the aircraft "glided" to recovery landing on a skid.

During the passage into the Magdeburg area, we were alerted with the "bogie" call and the intercom came alive with sightings of something diving down on us. The term bogie meant an unidentified aircraft approaching – something to watch. This bogie quickly became a "bandit," or hostile. Ferris in the top turret opened up with a burst or two and Pancoast went after him with the ball turret guns as the Me 163 passed through, but that was it. I saw nothing either before or after the attack, if one can describe it as such. We all marveled at the speed at which that bandit made his power-off sweep through our formation. While the Me 163 posed little danger, the jet powered Me 262 would prove to be a different matter. I never saw the 262 in any of my remaining missions except for contrails well above us and our fighter screen. There were no more bandits to confront the 487th on this day, but the flak would be waiting for us at Magdeburg. The flak was always waiting.

With the advent of our new B-17G, mission briefings would pump anxiety levels to new highs. Tensions ran high on the morning of 6 August at the mission briefing. After the previous day's mission to Magdeburg, I assumed apprehensively that the target would be somewhere in Germany – hopefully not Berlin or "Happy Valley." The curtain hiding the map was drawn back, and all eyes beheld the course line wandering northeastward up the North Sea along the Frisian Islands to Helgoland, an island just west of Bremerhaven. Helgoland served as a German naval base in both the world wars. From there, the course line swung to the east and plunged into the heart of Germany. Berlin was indeed the target, and groans of resignation filled the air, mine included. I remember looking across the room at my friend "Mac" McGinn to see his reaction. He seemed unmoved, but I knew his thoughts paralleled mine. For some reason I experienced a sense of foreboding, and I knew intuitively that my friend Clarence McGinn would not return that day.

The Eighth Bomber Command went after oil refineries, aircraft, munitions, and other factories in Germany on that day with over 1,000 B-17 and B-24 aircraft. Strikes involving 1,000 plus bombers were now common, and the numbers would continue to grow. Consider how much better the loss rate was in the summer of 1944 than a year earlier. On 6 August, the Eighth put up 1,186 aircraft of which 929 made their way effectively into the target areas. Of these, 24 were shot down and four more scrapped for a loss rate of

185

three percent. That number guaranteed nobody a ticket to survival, but it was a hell of a lot better than a year earlier. The survival outlook was much brighter. At the time, my mindset could hardly be influenced by calculated probabilities, since I had no inkling of what the big picture looked like. We were influenced only by the realities of what was happening around us.

With yet another clear day over the British Isles and continental Europe, the 487th formed over the airfield at a low altitude climbing en route over the North Sea toward Helgoland. As the group passed over the island, flak batteries positioned there opened up on us. We were still climbing when the exploding black bursts appeared around us. As Eubank flew the aircraft, my routine engine instrument scan wandered to the oil pressure gauge on number one – we were losing oil pressure even though the engine seemed to be operating normally. Drawing Chuck Eubank's attention to the pressure drop, he in turn advised Harry Ferris by intercom and brought him out of the top turret for a conference. As the pressure drop continued slowly but inexorably, we concluded that the oil tank for number one engine or the crankcase had been holed by flak and we were losing the engine oil supply. Unlike the B-24H, the B-17G oil tanks had no reserve standpipe that retained sufficient oil for feathering the propeller. For this reason, during our limited training on the B-17, great emphasis was placed on feathering before oil pressure was lost, otherwise the sequence could not be accomplished. The specter of another runaway propeller was very much part of our collective mindsets. Chuck, Harry, and I all realized that the problem could also be a faulty instrument. Chuck had to make the decision, but having little desire to see Berlin this day, or any other day for that matter, I secretly nudged him in thoughts toward feathering the prop. As the oil pressure needle approached the bottom line, Chuck punched the feathering button and shut down the ignition and fuel flow to number one. Gauge or not, it was a good decision. Had that engine failed approaching or leaving the target area, we would have fallen out of formation and been dead meat for the Luftwaffe. Ten good men wasted, like so many others.

With the group still climbing as it approached the German coastline, we were unable to keep pace and fell well behind the others. There was no hope of staying in formation on three engines if the group was still climbing to its assigned bombing altitude of 28,000 feet. I was ready to go home right then and there, but another one of those Dave Wilcox schemes surfaced and became the subject of a quick intercom conference. Chuck wasn't convinced that he had made the right decision, and his thoughts turned toward salvaging some sort of face-saving bombing sortie out of the aborted plan in case it was the instrument and not a depleted oil supply that led to shutting down the engine. That was all Dave Wilcox needed, except for one problem: no bombsight. Norden bomb sites were carried only in the lead and deputy lead aircraft in the 12 plane formation we were flying.

We had leveled off at an altitude of 12,000 feet while all this was going on and were still on an easterly heading. At Dave's direction, we continued east and crossed the German coast in search of a suitable "target of opportunity," as Frank Nelson and Dave poured over the maps. Dave convinced Chuck that if a large target such as an airfield could be found, he could "eyeball" the drop from our present altitude with at least an outside chance of hitting it. I thought the whole idea was insane, but in we went and found Nordholz airfield not too far inland from where we penetrated the coastline. Dave Wilcox did his thing with the bombs. We never knew where they hit mother earth since all had delayed action fuses, an exercise in futility if there ever was one.

Luckily, we picked up a P-51 escort fighter on the way back to the North Sea. Friendly fighter pilots were sensitive to the vulnerability of a lone bomber exiting enemy territory. We could see him as a speck in the distance, not sure initially whether he was friend or foe. This "Little Friend" approached us with great caution; he probably had his fill of being shot at by jumpy B-17 gunners. He made his approach very slowly, giving ample time for us to study the airframe's characteristics. Bf 109s and P-51s presented similar silhouettes at distances where they appeared as mere specks. Before getting in our gun range, Little Friend jettisoned his drop tanks after which we all breathed easily as he slid into position on our right wing. Little Friend got us home in good shape.

The idea that those randomly tossed bombs might have plunged into some German hamlet was a possibility we were very much aware of. We all rationalized to some extent that indiscriminate bombing was not part of the Eighth Air Force's war agenda. Targets we went after in Germany were related to that nation's industrial war munitions output – factories and oil production plants. Pinpoint bombing with surgical precision was the concept, but that capability existed only in theory and the minds of wartime propagandists who routinely fed us misinformation. Because we were young and naive, we accepted it. Yet even in our naiveté, we began to realize that we could never achieve such accuracy and knew full well that industrial targets in the hearts of German cities were surrounded by non-military/industrial activities.

The effectiveness of bombing results was measured by assessing in footage where the concentration of bombs fell in relation to the aiming point. Circles around the target were drawn in feet and referred to as "circles of error;" e.g., 1,000 feet, 1,500 feet, 2,000 feet, etc. Weather, poor target identification, and sloppy formation hampered effective bomb strike patterns. A bomb pattern was considered tight if the circle of error averaged 1,500 feet. Circles of error in visual bombing well over 2,000 feet were common. Some could be measured in miles, especially in cases where the squadron formation was strung out. Radar bombing, when introduced, would be even less accurate, greatly exacerbating the problem of confining the bomb pattern to the intended target. We therefore knew that a lot of innocent people died in our attacks. The rationalization for most (at least me) was that it was not our objective, and we pointed to the horrors of Rotterdam, Warsaw, Coventry, and London as examples of Germany's indiscriminate attacks on helpless city populations. The British with their carpet-bombing rationale and different objectives accepted this trade-off. Who could blame them after Coventry, the London Blitz, and the ensuing indiscriminate use of V1/V2 missiles? Nonetheless, the specter of massive destruction, firestorms, and the extermination of innocents would forever lie in the back of my mind as I matured.

Had we known about the German death camps at that juncture, the bombs we dropped on that day would have been delivered with vindictive justification. We knew nothing about them in July 1944, although our leaders had knowledge of their existence. Exploratory considerations were under review by the RAF to bomb these camps. Carl Spaatz had been approached by the RAF to mount a precision attack using the Norden site on the Auschwitz death camp, but wisely declined. Spaatz did not think he could accurately hit ovens and gas chambers without killing large numbers of inmates in surrounding buildings.

Guidelines we got from our leaders went something like this: Never drop indiscriminately in France or the Low Countries; in Germany, don't worry about it. Our task was to defeat Germany at whatever cost. Yet we all knew that innocent men, women, and children were dying in the infernos produced by our work.

On returning to Lavenham, I realized my intuitive feeling about Clarence McGinn proved to be correct. He and his crew went down over Berlin. About two weeks after he was shot down, I received a letter from McGinn's mother desperately seeking information as to his fate. I had no idea and penned a reply that I have regretted to this day. From what I could discern from others in the squadron who witnessed the event, his aircraft went down out of control after a direct hit on number two engine. Based on my inquiries and similar events that I had seen, I concluded erroneously that the crew probably did not get out of the aircraft and so informed Mrs. McGinn. My sense of the situation was that I did not want to give her false hopes. My negative mindset was conditioned very much by the unfriendly skies in which I then lived.

When I returned to New York in October, the first thing I did after debarking was find a phone to call Mrs. McGinn. I would learn for the first time that Mac was a prisoner of war as were the rest of the crew except the bombardier, Edward Reichel, who died of wounds after his capture. Years later, I learned from a surviving crew member that German medics refused to treat Reichel's debilitating wounds and simply let him die because he was a Jew. Mac told me that he himself landed in an open field. As he stripped away the chute and harness and tried to collect his wits, he saw a group of civilians running toward him from one direction, and soldiers from the opposite. Mac lacked nothing in intelligence; he turned and ran toward the soldiers and probably would not have lived to tell the story had he not done so.

On recovering at Lavenham well ahead of the rest of the 837th Squadron, we taxied to our hard stand and shut down the engines. As we were in the process of securing the aircraft, a jeep pulled up in front of the nose. In it was Russell Fisher, our original squadron commander, who had moved up in the management chain to become Group Executive Officer. Obviously, Fisher was suspicious about our reason for aborting the mission. Eubank had to explain in detail why we were home early, as well as our attack on Nordholtz airfield. We learned later from our crew chief, Sgt Brockhaus, that the oil gauge was faulty – there was nothing wrong with the engine, nor had the oil supply been depleted. Doing our bit to salvage the mission by bombing Nordholtz airfield got us no recognition, but at least we were not put on trial.

18 August 1944   Darky, Darky, Darky

Larry Herman called me in early on the morning of the 18 August and asked me to take a group of squadron mates to Edinburgh where they would have a few days of flak leave to enjoy the Scottish capital. One of the other 837th pilots would go with me, and we would split pilot-copilot duties. I would act as aircraft commander on the flight to Edinburgh, and he would do the return flight. The flight crew included an engineer and navigator. Our aircraft was a stripped down, war weary, F model of the B-17.

We departed Lavenham about noon in good weather with me at the controls. The flight to Edinburgh was uneventful except for the fact that I made a sorry landing, perhaps better described as a controlled crash. Bear in mind up to this point I had the princely sum of three hours flight training in the left seat of the B-17. I accumulated about 30 hours on five missions up to August 18, but all in the right seat. While I had gotten used to the flight characteristics of the G model, the landing idiosyncrasies of the F were unknown. There was some kind of spring in the control yoke elevator function peculiar to the F model that was apparently intended to stabilize the yoke when taxiing in ground operations. Pilots were advised to be wary of the yoke when reaching touchdown speeds on landing. Some poor slob always doesn't get the word. So my uneducated touchdown was such that the spring took over on contact with the runway and what followed was a B-17 performance worthy of a Sea World porpoise as it bounded down the runway, lurching to halt on the final bounce. Passengers to a man were all petrified, and I am sure the British in the Edinburgh control tower were rolling on the floor splitting with glee. What the hell, I thought, "any landing you can walk away from is a good landing."

We were in Edinburgh long enough to assure that the return trip would be at least partly at night in spite of the lingering daylight in those northern latitudes. There were no airways to fly and no navigational aids to facilitate an instrument orientation and approach to an unlighted airfield with no electronic landing aids – not even a coded light beacon. Our navigator was faced with a dead reckoning exercise with no map reference for a pilotage navigation fix, but he did have a Gee to determine actual position accurately. The flight was made over the length of a blacked out countryside – pitch black – with no light other than the stars above and the rosy glow of our engine exhaust collector rings. I was in the copilot's seat, somewhat grateful that I would not have to land this bestial F model, nor would the responsibility be mine if we got lost, a foreboding of which grew in my mind by the minute as I contemplated the uncertainties of the navigation situation. We flew to the point of our estimated time of arrival, and with Gee we knew we were near Lavenham and began circling. At this point, I tried to raise the Lavenham tower on the appointed VHF radio frequency with negative results. Repeated calls and frequency changes failed to produce the Lavenham landing circuit and runway lights, and it was becoming increasingly clear that we did not know where the hell we were. It turned out that Lavenham operations did not know we were inbound, and there was no one in the control tower.

Fortunately for us, the British had a system in place for handling lost souls in airplanes at night. It was called Darky. The routine went something like this: get on a VHF or HF emergency frequency and say "Darky, Darky, Darky, I'm lost, I'm lost, I'm lost." Yes, it had to be said three times and repeated three times. "This is so and so (call sign) requesting a DF (direction finding) steer to such and such." So I did the Darky bit three times as prescribed and asked for a DF steer to Lavenham. Within seconds the most wonderfully soothing English voice responded to our call sign and asked for a prolonged voice count through which a triangulation of our position could be made by him and two other Darky stations. It turned out we were practically over the airfield, and the Darky chap was also kind enough to raise the Lavenham tower by phone. Within minutes we had the blue circuit lights that outlined the circular air traffic flow right off our wing tip and made our approach and landing without further difficulty.

The Americans had no such procedure for recovering their bombers at night. Even though I would not get another chance in England to play transport pilot again, I concluded that I would leave the night flying to the British.

Peenemunde/Rechlin

My deepest penetration to a target in Germany was on 30 August. This, my 30th mission, was a strike against the German experimental station at Rechlin, part of the Peenemunde complex –famous as the seat of research and development of V1 and V2 weapons, as well as advanced aircraft designs. The Eighth dispatched over 1,200 heavies against aircraft plants, experimental stations, and synthetic oil factories. Of these, 380 were from my Third Air Division with assigned targets at Rechlin and Politz. [6]

Rechlin lies some 120 miles north of Berlin on the Baltic Sea. I remember this mission vividly – perfect weather with a long trek to and from the target across the Schleswig-Holstein peninsula. Flak in the target area was heavy, but we saw no enemy fighters anywhere along the route, which I thought was quite unusual and much to my liking. The 487th lost another aircraft due to a direct flak hit over the target. There were two survivors, the pilot 1st Lt Joseph Duncan and tail gunner S/Sgt Monroe Wolyn. The Third Division lost seven more aircraft on this mission, with one more written off and 182 damaged. Overall, the Eighth lost 21 planes with 336 suffering battle damage.

I cannot remember whether Rechlin was my first mission as aircraft commander. It was not unusual to use a seasoned copilot as a replacement for a sick or otherwise indisposed first pilot in filling out the crews for mission duty. Not all my missions were flown with Eubank. There were two occasions early in our combat tour where I stood down on missions so a green replacement pilot could get combat exposure with a veteran pilot.

As a footnote, in the 1970s while working in NASA Headquarters, I had occasion to meet and get to know Wehrner Von Braun. He had been reassigned to NASA Headquarters after a long stint in Huntsville, Alabama as the key figure in the development of our launch vehicle capability, most notably the Saturn rocket. Von Braun, of course, was also the pioneer of the German V2. During a meeting in NASA Headquarters one day, I ventured forth in good spirits, telling Dr. Von Braun that I had bombed Rechlin – the seat of V-1/V-2 development – on 25 August 1944. "See how much good you did?" he responded. We had a good laugh.

Hold Firm

CHAPTER 18   SEPTEMBER 1944: DUSSELDORF

Eighth Bomber Command operations in September 1944 were now revealed as something of an airborne colossus. In a sense, targeting had been following on the heels of the ground campaign in tactical support as our troops neared Germany's borders. But now the Eighth was back in the strategic bombing business big time. For 19 of September's 30 days, the U.S. launched major heavy bomber attacks on industrial targets in Germany with emphasis on oil production. Most of these missions were flown with close to or more than 1,000 heavy bombers accompanied by an strong force of fighter escorts.

During September, over 37,000 tons of bombs were dumped, mostly on German cities. The cost to the Eighth was high. There were monumental air battles as the German's dug in their heels. German defensive tactics also began to change with the introduction of their more heavily armed interceptors. Enemy action claimed 241 heavies lost, with battle damage to many more. Of these, 62 returned to their bases to be written off. The known cost in human casualties was 137 killed and 257 wounded who were returned to base. Most of the returned dead were buried in the American Cemetery at Cambridge. Sadly, the big human cost for September alone was 2,114 missing – dead, wounded, or prisoners.

Led by elements of the Third Air Division, on 1 September the Eighth Bomber Command launched 988 B-17s and B-24s to strike industrial targets in Germany. The effort was a bust, due to weather over the continent, and the mission was recalled. Only 16 "effectives" reached their objectives. Our target was Halach, Germany. While we never got anywhere near the target, we did penetrate enemy territory deep enough to get credit for the mission. I was delighted, only three to go.

Dusseldorf was the second first pilot assignment for me, again filling out a crew assembled by the squadron operations officer from available crewmen. By September of 1944 most of the aircrews that originally formed the 487th were beginning to break up as they neared the ends of their tours somewhat unevenly because of sickness, battle wounds, or whatever. Even more disruptive, some crewmen elected to fly the full 35 mission tour. Others opted for 30 missions with a stateside leave of 30 days after which they had to return for another combat tour. Except for 9 September, I cannot remember the name or face of a single crewmate I flew with in September. Manning the aircraft for missions was becoming a nightmare for the squadron operations officer.

August and September 1944 brought fresh focus to my parochial view of the air war in Europe. I now endured the flak somewhat stoically, but the threat of fighters made my heart beat rapidly as anxiety levels bordered on paranoia.

Der Sturmgruppen

In an issue of *The Baltimore Sun* some years ago, former Eighth Air Force pilot Ellis M. Woodward describes a German fighter attack that wiped out all but two aircraft of his 12-plane squadron formation. The article's headline states "Bomber Pilot Survived Attack by Secret Unit." In Woodward's words, "There were only us and our right wing man left. Our plane was shot to hell, but we made it back." Woodward's squadron was hit by the *Sturmgruppen*, the "secret" unit referred to in the *Sun*. Perhaps not that well known then, history has since accurately recorded their presence and impact. The Sturmgruppen took the gang attack techniques employed by the Luftwaffe to new heights.

The Sturmbock Fw 190s were armed with four wing mounted cannons – two 20mm and two 30mm. There were two fuselage-mounted machine guns and a drop tank for extended range. Armor plate and bullet resistant glass ringed the pilot for protection from our guns.

I learned of the Sturmgruppen in recent years, but had never previously read anything written by a recipient of their destructive power. The noted American artist Keith Ferris has done a painting he calls *Real Trouble* from which 1,000 prints were struck. I have no. 171 hanging in my collection. It depicts a formation of B-17s from a point above the formation, and at eye level in the scene is a gaggle of Fw 190 Sturmbock fighters poised for the attack. A squadron of Bf 109 escort fighters accompanies the 190s. The 190s were so heavy that they were no match for our Mustangs in a dogfight, thus the 109 escorts. The print came with details on the aircraft as well as the tactics. Suffice it to say that the weapon and its use were a formidable challenge for the Eighth Air Force.

The Sturmgruppen tactic emerging was called "The Company Front," and it proved highly effective against our heavy bomber formations. As many as 48 heavily armed and armored Fw 190s would close on our formations in waves of 8 to 16. The bombers receiving such attacks could be smothered with firepower and the formations frequently disrupted in a single firing pass. Had it not been for the escort fighters, it would have been 1943 all over again. The ranks of the bomber streams would have been pulverized.

On 9 September, Eighth Bomber Command launched another massive raid against targets in Western Germany – 1,212 heavies. 384 of these were the Eighth's Third Air Division B-17 groups including the 487th. Objectives for the Third Division were Dusseldorf, Leverkusen and Bonn. Our target was Dusseldorf right smack in the middle of the Ruhr – "Happy Valley" – a target complex noted for producing "flak happy" American airmen. I saw none of the Sturmgruppen that day, but I will give odds they hit somebody. Roger Freeman puts the Eighth's losses on 9 September at 19 aircraft lost or scrapped, 449 damaged, 20 crewmen killed or wounded in the air battles, and 150 missing in action. In terms of getting shot down, those are not bad odds considering the fact that over 1,000 bombers made successful drops. I note that the 390th Bomb Group suffered a high loss – 5 of their 36 aircraft – suggesting a Sturmgruppen attack.

September 9, 12 and 27 were fearful days for the Eighth Bomber Command, suggesting the effectiveness of Luftwaffe fighter tactics at this stage in the air war. The missions Woodward describes in *The Baltimore Sun* article were flown on September 12 and 27, 1944. In his extensive work *The Mighty Eighth*, Roger Freeman notes the 12 September mission listing all committed bomb groups, their targets, and their losses. Over 800 "effectives" dumped almost 2,000 pounds of bombs on industrial targets in Germany, mostly oil production facilities. Forty of these aircraft went down. Freeman shows Woodward's 493rd Bomb Group as losing 9 of their 36 aircraft. Woodward does not mention his group by number but notes his squadron as the 861st, which probably was one of four comprising the 493rd. Three of the four squadrons were probably committed to that mission; apparently two of the squadrons emerged unscathed. Woodwards' reference to the 27 September mission in which the 445th group lost 25 of 36 aircraft agrees with Freeman's count.

The introduction of the jet powered Messerschmitt 262 posed an even greater threat to the health of Eighth Air Force bomber crews than the Sturmgruppen. We had nothing to match the Me 262's performance. The Germans were never able to get enough of them into an effective defense posture because of Hitler's insistence that they be used as fighter-bombers, much to the chagrin of his air defense commander Adolf Galland. It was probably too late anyway, considering the breakthrough in the ground campaign.

Galland's utter frustration with Goering's use of the 262 reached rebellious proportions as the war neared its end.

In retrospect, Dusseldorf was among the most interesting missions I flew because of the irony and emotions we experienced as a crew. For Chuck and the others it would be their last mission. For me, two more remained. As a crew, we flew most missions together – Eubank and the others had flown 34; my count was 32.

One thing our leaders tried to do for crews finishing their combat tours was to assign them a "milk run" for their last mission. On 9 September Frank and the others were scheduled to fly their 35th and last mission, but it was my name that came up on the mission board instead of Chuck's. He was assigned as my copilot. I can't remember exactly why that was the case, but at this point I was flying as an aircraft commander and due for a mission. More likely is the fact that I was being prepared for a crew assignment by Larry Herman. Chuck was without a copilot and had one more to fly, so Larry Herman decided to put us together. Because it was not my last mission, no allowance was made for degree of target difficulty even though it was the final mission for the remainder of the crew. The target could not have been more formidable – Dusseldorf in the heart "Happy Valley." I vividly recall the scene preceding Lutzkendorf in the big Nissan building that served as our briefing room. The curtain was, as usual, drawn away from the large map exposing the planned flight path. Drawn in a heavy line, it originated in East Anglia and wandered around expected flak concentrations in Belgium and West Germany and thence into the heart of the Ruhr. Needless to say, there was that "we was robbed" reaction, with me griping as loudly as anyone – not Dusseldorf! But our protests were to no avail. The worst thing for Eubank and the others was the dread that went with having to do it for the last time and all the "what ifs" that went along with that feeling. My God, the target was Dusseldorf in clear weather without much chance of a recall. Maybe we would lose an engine on the way in, just deep enough to credit a mission. To be sure, it was time for white knuckles and wet palms. I had three more missions to fly, so I was not any more up tight than usual.

We made our way from the briefing room to the aircraft hard stand where I went through my usual watch and ring routine with Sgt. Brockhaus. Before each mission, I would take off my watch and ring and give it to Brockhaus who was, in my mind, a mentor. By now it had grown from the simple desire to leave memorabilia with my family to a superstition. Because I had gotten back from all the other missions having done this, I would not consider climbing in that aircraft without giving those items to Brockhaus.

With my ritual of survival fulfilled, now came the long wait under the wing in the emerging daylight with the knot growing in my stomach as the minutes passed. Would we get a green flare or a red one? God, let it be red so I can live another day. I did not want to go to Dusseldorf. Dark thoughts always invaded my soul at such moments – the enemy flak and fighters, the mid-air collisions. If those hazards did not end it, the German civilians would tear you to pieces. Who could blame them? It seems so ironic as I look back; imagine how that knot in my stomach would have felt had I known of the havoc the Sturmgruppen could wreak on our formations.

The flare was green, and we made our way to our respective crew positions. Chuck and I, Frank, Willie, and Harry all entered through the forward hatch located at the bottom of the fuselage just under the flight deck. Entry through this hatch was a sort of athletic ritual. Loose gear was tossed up through the opening first. Hands were then placed on the port side of the hatch with a palms up grip. Legs were then swung up into the hatch first with the rest of the body following – head last.

Chuck swung through the opening first as he always did, and I followed. Even though I had been designated aircraft commander for the mission, out of respect for Chuck when we reached the flight deck I climbed into the copilot's seat. After all, it was Chuck's crew, not mine. I was an integral part of the original crew, and decided to take my usual spot. Perhaps this was another symbol of the way we had bonded.

Eubank's usual reserve and unemotional demeanor were very much evident as we went through the checklist. On this day, however, he was quieter than ever. He was suffering with a heavy cold, and what with the prospects that lay before us he was quite miserable, but determined to fly this last mission. Come to think of it, his physical condition that day may have been the main reason I was designated aircraft commander. We said nothing to one another except for my reading of the checklist and Chuck's responses as we prepared to start engines and taxi out into our assigned place in the pre-take-off line. Chuck made the take-off, and we assembled visually in the clear morning air over the airfield. I did most of the flying after assembly from the right seat, looking across the cockpit at the right wing tip of the element leader. I would become married to that wing tip for the next few hours with intermittent relief periods provided by Chuck as I tired. It was the focal point of my concentration, and my eyes would rarely leave it. Such were the demands of formation flying.

The intercom would usually be alive with crew chatter on these missions, but there was hardly a peep out of anybody on that airplane as we approached the target area. The IP where we would turn on the bomb run was just south of Dusseldorf. There, the column of B-17 groups comprising the bomber stream would break into squadrons for the attack. As we neared the IP I caught glimpses of the heavy flak barrage lying in wait for us over the city.

The 837th Squadron made its turn over the IP and fell in behind the lead squadron. Other units ahead were now engulfed in the flak barrage. But as we approached Dusseldorf, as if ordained by some divine being, the flak barrage ended abruptly. This apparently occurred because German fighters were in the area and about to attack. German flak batteries routinely held their fire when advised of impending attacks on our formations by their fighters. We never saw any of them, and the 837th emerged unscathed. Once again, God seemed to come to our defense, as if simply deciding that we had all suffered enough and just turned off the flak and told the fighter pilots to get lost. We got our "milk run" after all.

On the way home, the crew exploded – every one of them except me – with a new lease on life. Although most of Chuck's face was hidden behind his oxygen mask, I could clearly detect a smile dancing in those flu-laden, bleary eyes. It was an unforgettable day. As they all whooped and yelled, I sat there with the stark realization that I still faced that last mission.

There were several days of inactivity after the 9 September mission, which left me in a state of limbo as far as the squadron was concerned. I discussed this with the 487th Squadron CO, Maj John Hammett, and Capt Larry Herman, the squadron operations officer. I wanted to explore my prospects of going on to fighter training in England.

At the time a vital appendage to Eighth Bomber Command was the Scouting Force, an array of fighters fully combat ready and utilized for reconnaissance. The Scouting Force was created by Col Bud J. Peaslee, commander of the 384th Bombardment Group who recognized the vital need to check anti-aircraft sites over the continent in advance of the bomber streams and provide weather information for assembly, especially situations where bombers would take off under a deck of clouds, climb through it and assemble "on top." Bomber pilots had to know where the "top" was for a visible assembly above the clouds.

There were three components: Scouting Force 1 equipped with P-51s and P-38s attached to the 364th Fighter Group; Scouting Force 2 equipped with P-47s and P-51s attached to the 355th Fighter Group, and Scouting Force 3 equipped with P-47s, P-51s and a few B-17Fs attached to the 55th Fighter Group. During its six-month lifetime the Scouting Force lost 24 pilots: nine in training accidents and 15 in combat. Although the Scouting Force 3 was never meant for combat, the unit downed 22 Luftwaffe fighters in actions involving our bombers under attack.

Scouting Force pilots were assigned from the fighter groups to which they were attached, but many pilots like me, who had longed to fly fighters, volunteered for cross training and assignment to one of the scouting units. Hammett and Herman acknowledged that I had volunteered, but we all agreed that I should finish my 35 missions before moving on.

Herman asked me if I had ever taken any "flak leave." I replied in the negative. None of the Eubank crew took any leave, preferring instead to get the mission tour behind us as quickly as possible. Since there was nothing for me to do, the CO suggested I take a week's break in Bournemouth, a resort town on the Channel coast. He expected to have a crew for me on my return.

The next day I was flown to an airfield near the Channel coast and made my way to Bournemouth in some conveyance I cannot hope to remember. Several of us Eighth Air Force types were there at the same time. We were put up in a lovely hotel in a resort environment. There was little to do except to walk around and just hang out. My stay lasted about a week – perhaps a day or two longer, but it did span a weekend. It was during this stay in Bournemouth that I had to face the reality of two more missions, and the notion began to grow in my mind, perhaps brought on by the abrupt idleness I found in strange surroundings. The idea of survival from mission to mission had, over the course of my combat tour, surmounted and dominated the thought process. As the Bournemouth interlude unfolded, my day-by-day mood descended further into dark thoughts as I tried to cope with returning to fly those last two missions.

Thus far my flak leave was more of a curse than a blessing, and I was ready to leave after a few days.

I returned to Lavenham by train through London, Ipswich, and Bury St. Edmund. I arrived at the Bury station in the evening at about 8:00 p.m., but in plenty of time to run by the Athenaeum to see what might be going on there. The place was swinging as usual, full of military people both male and female, all in uniform, but mostly American airmen from nearby bases. I ran into Jim O'Connor who was one of my hut mates. He said that he had heard that I was going home. I shunted that idea aside telling him that it was unlikely since I had two missions yet to fly.

I left the Athenaeum close to midnight and took the usual "six by" truck back to the base and that little corner of the hut I occupied. No sooner had I climbed on top of those three "biscuits" that masqueraded as a mattress, I was roused out rudely by a pack of drunks who wanted me to join their revelry. "You're going home," they told me. In fact they all had orders to go home, and my name was on the orders. I had to see the document before I would believe it, but there it was: Special Order so and so, a bunch of names including Nolan, Bernard T. 1st Lt 0-816348 ordering me to a staging area where I would be "processed" to await transportation back to the states. Foregoing the party, I got up and started packing my footlocker and B-4 bag. I picked up my orders at 0800 that morning, signed out, and was gone, leaving my bicycle in its stand and whatever other paraphernalia that I could not stuff in my baggage.

Gone in an instant were all thoughts of going on to P-51 transition training and the Scouting Force. It was the trade-off of my life. I knew now that I would never have to fly that last mission, and there was no way I would hang around and let somebody change his mind. To hell with the P-51. The bottom line: the stress I was anticipating departed in a flash.

Although I expected more combat in the Far East, my combat days were actually behind me. Of course, the war went on for the 487th and the Eighth Air Force. Eight more months of punishing combat lay ahead. The 487th lost 5 aircraft and crews in September 1944, 2 in October, 6 more in November, and 12 in December. Among the November casualties was Loye Lauraine, one of the original 837th Squadron pilots and my hut mate through my entire experience at Lavenham. Lauraine was on his second combat tour having opted for 30 missions and a leave of absence in the U.S., from which he would return to England for a second combat tour. On November 25 he managed to get his heavily damaged B-17 back to the U.K. from Merseburg, Germany, but the aircraft was barely controllable and unable to land safely. Lauraine elected to evacuate his crew by parachute near Framlingham, Suffolk after which he would head the aircraft out to sea and bale out. He never made it.

Nine of the 12 aircraft lost went down on Christmas Eve in a single raid on Babenhausen, Germany, the result of German fighter attacks. Six of the 9 belonged to one of the 4 squadrons in the air that day – the 836th – strongly suggesting an Fw 190 attack by the Sturmgruppen. My old squadron, the 837th, lost none. It was the worst fighter attack the 487th experienced in its wartime tenure with the Eighth Air Force.

In mid-December the Wehrmacht poured through the Ardennes Forest in a last ditch effort to split the Allied ground forces and take the port of Antwerp, essential to their logistics support. What ensued was the Battle of the Bulge. The Germans' timing was perfect – to some extent serendipitous – due in any case to the foul weather covering Western Europe that denied allied air support. However, by 23 December the weather began to clear and it was possible to bring superior Allied air power to bear in support of our ground operations. On Christmas Eve the Eighth Bomber Command launched the largest force of bombers ever sent on a single day's operation against enemy targets in response to Hitler's last desperate offensive. Every available B-17 and B-24 would participate; even unarmed training aircraft were to be fed into the air strike. This maximum effort was tied directly to the ground fighting in the Battle of the Bulge and was designed to isolate the battlefield with visual strikes against communications targets and airfields in West Germany.

The 4th Air Combat Wing (the designation had been changed from the 92nd when a third group had been added) of the Third Air Division was selected to lead the mission. BGen Fred Castle, commander of the 4th, in turn chose my 487th as the lead group. Castle would personally fly in the 487th's lead aircraft.

Frederick Castle was a quiet, dignified man in his mid-thirties when he joined Ira Eaker's small staff of seven in England in February 1942 to lay the groundwork for what would become the Eighth Air Force. Then a captain, his exceptional abilities honed at West Point identified him as a rising star. He became Eaker's Chief of Staff for Supply and fulfilled that role ably in the difficult build-up period for the Eighth, but his desire for a combat command went unabated until he was given command of the 94th Bomb Group in June 1943. At the time the 94th and 97th were part of a new wing, and they had notorious reputations for poor performance and low morale among their airmen. Command of the 97th Group went to Frank Armstrong. It will be recalled in Beirne Lay's *Twelve O'clock High* that the central theme of the story deals with an Eighth Air Force group having a history of poor performance in combat, broken morale, and undisciplined airmen. A BGen named Savage

(Gregory Peck) is sent to whip them into shape. It has been said that Beirne Lay and his co-author Sy Bartlett modeled Savage after Frank Armstrong. Better models could not have been fictionally conceived. Both Castle and Armstrong were model leaders, cast in the mold of those few men who have the aggressive imagination, discipline, and commitment to rise to the challenge in warfare. They were most of all "hands-on" people, willing to pull from the front rather than push from the rear by flying in the lead aircraft.

Over 2,000 B-24s and B-17s were dispatched on December 24, and 850 escort fighters, mostly P-51s, covered them. The mission was flawed to some extent as it unfolded. Timing at rendezvous points was off, and the lead elements of the bomber stream were approaching the battle lines without their fighter escort. The 487th was attacked by a group of Bf 109s while still over friendly territory with no escort fighters on hand to challenge them. Castle's aircraft was piloted by 1st Lt. Robert Harriman; Castle was in the copilot's seat as the airborne commander of the mission. I have talked to three surviving ball turret gunners in other aircraft who witnessed the event. Henry Hughey occupied the ball turret of the aircraft on Castle's left wing and had a ringside seat. According to Hughey, the Bf 109s made their run head on. W.A. (Mike) Quering and Warren Buxton, ball turret gunners in other aircraft in the formation, agree. There were hits all over Castle's aircraft wounding several crewmembers and setting two engines on fire. Castle ordered the crew out of the aircraft, and he is given credit for taking the controls from Harriman giving him and the others the opportunity to bail out. Harriman never made it; he would die with Fred Castle in the ensuing explosion and crash. Five crewmen survived. Two others made it out but died later of wounds. Castle was awarded the Congressional Medal of Honor posthumously for his sacrifice.

Fred Castle's story of heroism is very special to people like me who were members of the 487th, and to this day we honor his memory. Hardly a household name here in the U.S., as the war fades from view, Castle is remembered in England. In Lavenham's Guildhall museum there is a tribute to him, and the Swan's pub still honors his name. The USAF honored him after the war by naming an air base for him.

In one sense, Fred Castle's sacrifice and Medal of Honor recognize all of the Eighth Air Force bomber crewmen who gave their lives. Yet the process of awards and recognition was arbitrary and flawed for many. Bear in mind that Robert Harriman, pilot of the aircraft in which Castle flew as air leader, perished with him. It was probably Harriman at the controls who fought to stabilize the aircraft while the crew evacuated. Loye Lauraine's actions to save his crew on 25 November were no less heroic. I have never been able to determine whether Harriman or Lauraine received any specific recognition for their heroism. Dave Wilcox's ingenuity on our June 1944 Châteaudun mission went unrecognized. I was awarded the Distinguished Flying Cross simply because I survived.

The annals of the Eighth's combat history are no doubt filled with such stories. For all the tales of glory and those of cowardice – or those who copped out to Sweden or Switzerland – one essential truth testifies to the performance of this grand air army: the Eighth may have been turned back by weather, but it was never turned back by enemy defenses. The vision of a 2,000-bomber raid is hardly imaginable in today's world. Both the sheer size of this bomber force and its persistence in the daylight campaign against Germany are what made it The Mighty Eighth.

Me 262 Schwalba (S wallow)

CHAPTER 19   DAS ENDE

The Luftwaffe had been ground down by 6 June and had mounted no significant opposition of Allied forces in the Normandy landings. But the Luftwaffe was far from out of business thanks to Adolf Galland and Albert Speer, Hitler's mastermind of German wartime industrial output.

Adolf "Dolfo" Joseph Ferdinand Galland was a man endowed by his creator with many gifts – a superb airman with a creative mind and another of the hands-on leaders who left an indelible imprint as both an aviator and as the *General der Jagdflieger* – leader of the Luftwaffe Fighter Command in WW II. I sensed these qualities when we talked that night at The National Air and Space Museum. At the time of that encounter I knew little about Galland, but as my research gives me insights into the man's character, I liken him and his gifts to the creativity of Jimmy Doolittle and the aggressiveness of Curtis LeMay. Like them, he had an intuitive understanding of the dynamics of aerial warfare and its complexities.

Born in 1912, Galland began his aviation career as a glider pilot, as did so many Luftwaffe pilots in WW II. It was that era when the Versailles Treaty barred Germany from having a military air force. Hitler would resolve that problem with alternatives such as gliders and powered flight training in Russia. At length he would simply ignore the treaty, and a resurgent Luftwaffe was born. Galland progressed to power flight training and obtained a B2 certificate in 1932. Beginning in 1933 he was flying Lufthansa airliners. During the Spanish Civil War, Galland was flying ground attack missions in the Condor Legion in a Henkel He 51. He flew 300 combat missions in Spain, devising new ground attack tactics. Ernst Udet, the second-highest scoring German flying ace of WW I, used his experience with pinpoint bombing in the development of the Ju 87

Stuka dive-bomber. Galland flew in the Polish campaign and in the May 1940 German incursions into France and the Low Countries.

During the air battle over Dunkirk, Galland met the Supermarine Spitfire for the first time and was deeply impressed by the performances of both the aircraft and its RAF pilot.

From June 1940 on, Galland flew as commander of Jagdgeschwader 26 (JG 26) fighter unit in the Battle of Britain for which he earned the coveted Knight's Cross of the Iron Cross with Oak Leaves, Swords and Diamonds." In the chaotic air encounters that followed, Galland was impressed by the Spitfire's ability to outmaneuver the Bf 109 in tight turns, the essential ingredient in getting off an effective deflection burst on an adversary. But Galland was a natural, and by December 1940 he had amassed 57 victories, the number one German ace, now ahead of his rival and friend Werner Moelders.

By the autumn of 1941 he had 96 victories, at which time he was poised for higher command and was ordered to fly no further combat missions. In November 1941, Herman Goering chose Galland as General der Jagdgeflieger to replace Werner Moelders, who had been killed in an air crash en route to attend the funeral of Ernst Udet.

Galland had the misfortune to lead Fighter Command as Germany fought on many fronts – Hitler's invasion of Russia, North Africa, and later Italy. With the United States now in the war with its industrial might, America and Britain built an armed vise that would eventually crush Germany. Perceiving such threats from the air, Galland recognized the need to upgrade the *Jagdwaffe* fighter aircraft for what would become the Defense of the Reich campaign. In his position as General der Jagdflieger he was not permitted to fly combat sorties, but did so anyway to familiarize himself with the Fw 190 now on the scene as well as with interception tactics.

As the war continued, his position also brought him into conflict with Herman Goering, as one might expect, considering the fact that Goering failed to grasp the fundamentals of aerial combat in the skies of WW II as early as the Battle of Britain. Divergent views of engagement tactics had already surfaced in the Battle with Goering's insistence that Bf 109 escorts stay with bombers en route to targets in Britain, precisely the wrong tactic, as we noted in Chapter 3. Later issues regarding the use of the Me 262 would drive them much further apart. Galland was no sycophant – he was outspoken, a quality not tolerated by Goering. In his efforts to expand the Jagdwaffe, he found ways to cultivate lions of German industry such as Albert Speer.

Hermann Goering was, of course, a key player in the wartime scenario, well before he was immersed in the Nazi political hierarchy. Born in 1893, he was the son of a former cavalry officer and diplomat. Goering's military service began in WW I from which he emerged as a veteran ace fighter pilot with 22 credited victories and recipient of the Pour le Merite. He also served as the last commander of the famed von Richtofen Jagdgeschwader 1 as the war ended. His membership in the Nazi party dates from its early days. He was wounded in the renowned beer hall *putsch* in 1923, when Hitler and others attempted to seize power in Munich, and Goering subsequently and permanently became addicted to morphine, given to him to ease the pain of his injuries. By 1923 Goering was well up the ladder of Nazidom. Goering was a founder of Hitler's Gestapo and was appointed to command the evolving Luftwaffe in 1935, a position he would occupy until the latter days of WW II. In 1941 Hitler conferred the rank of *Reichsmarschall* on Goering, the highest rank of the Nazi armed forces, elevating him above all Wehrmacht commanders. His star, however, was in decline as early as 1942, due to the Luftwaffe's defeats in battle and inability to meet its objectives, following which Goering's command presence became increasingly that of a meddlesome figurehead. Hitler relieved him as Reichsmarschall in April 1945.

Goering and Galland met in October 1943 as RAF bombers were pulverizing German cities and the Eighth Air Force was steadily building strength and penetrating deeply into German air space, albeit at a high cost in casualties.

Arguments between the two became intense over development issues, mainly inappropriate armament to be installed in the Me 410 and its performance flaws. Goering lapsed into attacks on the Jagdwaffe, accusing Galland's pilots of cowardice as he had during the Battle of Britain, and as he would do again late in the war. Arguments between Goering and Galland over aircraft procurement, armament and deployment would increasingly deepen the wedge between the two, bordering on Galland's eventually backing his pilots in rebellion.

By late 1944 Goering was out of favor with Hitler and became even more hostile toward Galland, holding him and his fighter pilots responsible for not effectively engaging incoming formations through the Low Countries into Germany. By the time of Big Week and Overlord, Galland's Jagdwaffe was exhausted; Galland told Goering that he had lost 1,000 pilots in four weeks and was heavily outnumbered by Allied fighters. Galland got no response.

The RAF and Eighth Air Force bombing operations ground on relentlessly with the Jagdwaffe increasingly held to account by Goering. The massive raids of 1,000 plus aircraft in bomber streams fanning out to multiple targets in Germany were now unstoppable, a fact realized by Galland, which led him to Albert Speer and a resurgence of fighter production. Galland's plan, known as *Grosser Schlag* (Big Blow), was to confront incoming bomber formations with a massive force of jet and propeller fighters. as many as 2,000. Some 2,500 Me 262s were produced and fielded thanks to Speer. How a defending force of this size would be controlled and vectored to the intercept is not clear. Perhaps a German replica of Hugh Dowding might have helped with the plans for implementation. Kammhuber, the German genius who developed Germany's integrated system of defense against bombing – day and night, the Kammhuber Line – was already put out to pasture.

While the fighters were available, pilot availability was suspect. By this time, their availability – especially for experienced pilots – had declined markedly due to casualties and training constraints imposed by fuel shortages. The Big Blow was never launched. Jagdwaffe fighters were instead committed to supporting German forces in the Battle of the Bulge. Ground support operations for the German army proved to be a disastrous failure, due largely to the blanket of low clouds that lay over the battlefield for weeks. On 13 January 1945, Adolf Galland was relieved of his command after protesting the operation and criticizing Goering too vigorously. That event galvanized Galland's fighter pilot peers to near revolt. In a worst case for Goering, he again accused his own fighter pilots of cowardice – criticism from a man who had not flown nor even led a combat mission in WW II, typical of the leader who pushes from the rear. Payback for Goering was bitter resentment.

The back breaker in the ensuing conflict between Goering, Galland and his supporters revolved around the Me 262. Hitler saw the aircraft as a bomber that, in concert with his V weapons, was capable of inflicting vindictive retribution on Britain. Goering, ever the sycophant, supported Hitler's position. Already convinced that Germany had lost the war, and after having actually flown the 262, Galland concluded that the aircraft as an air defense fighter had the potential of inflicting major disruption on Allied bombing operations and perhaps was even the key to Germany's survival.

Their country's survival was all that the Jagdwaffe pilots had left to fight and die for.

In his book *The Final Hours*, Johannes Steinhoff tells of a face-to-face meeting with Adolf Hitler that best illustrates the latter's position regarding aircraft production and the combat role of the Me 262. In July 1944, WW II fighter ace Steinhoff was summoned to Wolfshcanze, Hiller's headquarters in Poland, to receive the Sword's pendant to his Knight's Cross Oak Leaf Cluster. On his arrival at the headquarters complex, Stienhoff was taken aback by the changes in the environment and described the Fuehrer as looking like a worn out old man. Hitler proceeded straightaway to avow that the Reich must call a halt to Allied "terror" bombing – it had to be stopped. Hitler added that he wanted to hear the truth from the men at the front. Waxing on, Hitler noted that American and British fighters were faster, could fly higher, and were more maneuverable. Sensing an opportunity, Steinhoff ventured, "we need new and better aircraft, I was thinking of the jet fighter." In Hitler's now agitated, response, he accused people of going behind his back to put pressure on him. Steinhoff pressed on, adding that he had flown the Me 262 and regarded it a magnificent aircraft. Hitler, now further agitated, said that he didn't want to hear anymore of such nonsense, that his doctor had warned him that flying at such speeds in fighter maneuvers would set up enormous acceleration forces, causing blackouts. Like Goering, Hitler had no understanding of the combat environment planned for the 262; it did not call for dog fighting. Hitler said he did not want to hear another word, and that he had plans to mobilize the nation in ways yet unheard of: "I shall repay terror with terror," (*The Final Hours*, page 56).

Fatty's Got To Go

While the combat role of the Me 262 drove so much of the

wrangling among the key players, it was the unabated resentment among Luftwaffe airmen in the "Pilots' Revolt" that morphed into a conspiracy led by two of Galland's decorated combat leaders, Johannes Steinhoff and Gunther Luetzow. Steinhoff was a veteran fighter pilot with 176 victories. Command assignments included JG 52 and JG 77. In December 1944, *Oberst* (colonel) Steinhoff took command of the Me 262 equipped JG 7. He was subsequently relieved of that command by Goering due to his leadership role in the Fighter Pilots' Revolt, discussed below.

Steinhoff was then posted to a new experimental unit JV 44 by Adolf Galland, where he recorded 6 victories flying the Me 262. In April 1945, Steinhoff was horribly burned in the crash of an Me 262 on an aborted take off. He bore the facial scars caused by burns for the rest of his life, as did many other crash survivors of countries involved in the air war. In a post war career with the rebuilt Luftwaffe, Steinhoff rose to its post war leadership from 1966 to 1970. He served as Chairman of the NATO Military Committee from 1971 to 1974.

Guenther Luetzow was another decorated Luftwaffe ace with 110 credited victories. Like Steinhoff, he held both the Knight's Cross and Iron Cross. Luetzow was at the core of Luftwaffe dissension (the Fighter Pilots' Revolt) along with Steinhoff. He joined Galland's JV 44 and recorded two victories before going missing on April 24, 1945. His body was never recovered. Goering regarded both Steinhoff and Luetzow as mutineers.

In his book *The Final Hours*, Steinhoff records Goering's bizarre behavioral personality, as well as the root causes of his airmen's discontent. In mid-November 1944, Steinhoff was ordered to attend a two-day meeting to be held under the chairmanship of Goering at airbase Berlin Gatow. Awaiting the Reichmarschall's appearance in the conference room, Steinhoff noted that he was in distinguished company – "heroes" to a man. Luetzow was also in attendance. Goering entered the room like a bloated peacock, baton in jeweled hand, dressed in his dove gray double-breasted uniform with the wide silk lapels. He announced that he expected critical discussion about how the service could be improved, criticisms, however, to stop short himself. He went on to deplore the "dwindling morale" and "fruitless wrangling" over the use of the Me 262 as a bomber or fighter. And on it went as Steinhoff reports in his book: "I want you to give the Luftwaffe back its reputation because we have failed disgracefully. This is the Luftwaffe's darkest hour. The nation cannot understand why Allied bombers can come waltzing over the Reich as they did on the very day of our party congress and the fighters do not take off – because of fog, or because they are not ready or because they are indisposed." After the diatribe, Goering stated that he had other commitments and had to leave, announcing before his departure that Galland had been elevated in rank to *Generalleutnant*, to which Galland muttered later, "bad sign, that means it won't be long before they sling me out." The criticisms and discussion for improvements were then turned over to an underling.

A month earlier, Goering called together key commanders of bomber and fighter command and delivered the same tirade, accusing his fighter pilots of inflating claims with lies and with cowardice – the humiliating indictment this time delivered to the entire Luftwaffe. Luetzow and Steinhoff were witnesses to these events; both had to sit and take it. They came to the conclusion that they had to act, that they owed it to their comrades, who continued to climb into their aircraft and fight, ever faithful to their country, regardless of the fact that most conceded the war was lost.

Both events best illustrate the climate of resentment bordering on hatred that gave birth to the Pilots' Revolt. Luetzow put it on the table: "We've got to do something, Macky [familiar name for Steinhoff]. One thing is certain now – Fatty's got to go!" On 17 January 1945 the conspiracy cadre met and formulated a list of demands for the survival of the Jagdwaffe, with the ultimate objective of deposing Hermann Goering. But what would they do with this listing of demands? Goering refused to meet with them and had already regarded both Luetzow and Steinhoff as mutineers. Both were now marked men, along with Adolf Galland. Goering was the number two man in the Nazi hierarchy – the conspirators knew they would have to get to Hitler to depose him. That seems unlikely at first glance, but they would press on nonetheless. Recognizing the futility of using official channels to reach a direct audience with Hitler, Luetzow and Steinhoff decided to approach the *Schutzstaffel* (Hitler's Defense Corps), called the SS, and ask them to arrange an interview. The also knew that the SS approach would be risky, given Himmler's idea of bringing the German military under the aegis of the SS. The decision was made to go forward with an SS officer known to one of the cabal – an *Obergruppenfuhrer* (senior group leader) familiar with Luftwaffe issues who might be helpful. The group, led by Luetzow, met with the Obergruppenfuhrer on 4 January 1945. What they got was an interrogation laced with Nazi party rhetoric. The scene could not have been worse. Luetzow left the Obergruppenfuhrer with a parting: "it was five minutes to midnight." The response was, "It's five minutes to victory," when the Fuhrer would mobilize the nation and bomb Britain with V-1s and V-2s. Summarily dismissed by the Obergruppenfuhrer, Lutzow and Steinhoff were back out on the street of futility.

On 13 January the rebel pair made their way to Generaloberst (colonel general) Ritter von Greim's Third Air Fleet Headquarters in Litzmannstadt, Poland to seek sympathetic ears for their case against Goering. Von Greim was a highly regarded fighter pilot in WW I – both likeable and approachable. He invited Lutzow and Steinhoff to attend the evening's situation report meeting that focused on the exploding Russian offensive. The Russian thrust was not unexpected, but its ferocity and strength were – perhaps "the beginning of the end." Von Greim listened patiently to the litany of grievances presented by Luetzow and asked him what he proposed to do about it. Steinhoff offered in reply the basic plan to concentrate massive and coordinated fighter action to stop incoming bomber attacks on German cities, also adding the resentment that prevailed in Jagdwaffe over Goering's accusations of cowardice. Steinhoff went on to ask von Greim if he would be prepared to replace Goering, and that the matter should be brought before Hitler.

Von Greim's response was now negative, allowing that Goering's favor with the Fuhrer had been in decline for some time. Hitler had already brought von Greim on board as his Luftwaffe advisor, but also thought Goering should be retained as its nominal head. The Reichmarshall was aware of the situation. Greim was unwilling to take the matter forward, and suggested that the case be presented to General Koller, Chief of the Luftwaffe General Staff.

On 17 January Luetzow and Steinhoff were summoned to meet with Koller who had already been alerted to their demands. Both now realized that their attempts to reach Hitler had ended. What was left was to confront Goering directly. The meeting with Koller was two days later with Luetzow again presenting the grievances. Koller cut them off, stating that their views and demands amounted to conspiracy, if not outright mutiny. But he did agree to arrange a face-to-face meeting with Goering.

That meeting would take place a few days later with Koller in attendance. Koller reminded Goering that he had written to advise him that a number of his group commanders had asked for a frank discussion with him. Koller went on to introduce Luetzow as spokesman. Luetzow, composed and not intimidated, proceeded with the recitation of grievances and demands. With Goering initially listening passively, the meeting gradually became another shouting match. Goering finally exploded, saying he had had enough. He threatened to have Luetzow shot, and with a wave of his bejeweled hand stomped out of the room. Luetzow and Steinhoff finally faced up to the reality of what was to follow – detention, stripping of decorations, and courts martial. But nothing happened, and rabid tensions finally slipped into memory. Thus ended the Fighter Pilots' Revolt. But the war raged on.

Steinhoff met with Adolf Galland following the Goering blow out, the latter advising him that the Reichmarschall had ordered that Steinhoff was not to command a flying unit and that he would be advised of his next posting. Meantime, Steinhoff was to stand down. Luetzow was now gone, having been posted to a fighter group in Italy. Galland said further that his sense of the situation was that "Fatty" would never forgive him, and that he, Galland, was regarded as the ringleader.

Hitler had been advised of the fighter pilot uproar and Galland's status by Albert Speer, who told him that Galland was in fighter pilot's limbo. Hitler's response was that Galland should be able to prove that the Me 262 is a fighter – "give him a unit." Goering offered Galland the cheapest solution – a squadron. Galland accepted what would become Fighter Unit 44 to be based at Brandenburg. He went on to recruit the crème de la crème of Luftwaffe fighter pilots, including Steinhoff and Luetzow, recalled from Italy.

Galland's lost strategy, it will be recalled, was to confront bomber formations with massive fighter power – as many as 80 Me 262s accompanied by Me 109s and Fw 190s. What he would learn from developing tactics by Fighter Unit 44's limited engagements was that the strategy might have been effective in curtailing or even ending bomber attacks. In waves, the 262s could fly through escorting fighter screens (they could not be overtaken) to disrupt and disburse the formations, thereby allowing his propeller driven fighters to pick off the stragglers. The concept was never fully proven, but its potential was demonstrated by Galland's pilots. Fighter Unit 44 initially operated from Brandenburg, but late in March 1945, Galland decided to move the unit to Bavaria in order to protect what was left of the aircraft industry. Operations were set up at the Munich-Riem airfield where the Me 262s could be in the best position to intercept Eighth Air Force B-17s and B-24s. Operations were limited at best – a maximum effort might get 9 Me 262s airborne. Eighth Air Force Mustangs and Lightnings also stalked the airfield, knowing that the 262's take off and landing performances made them sitting ducks in a shooting gallery. Pilots, veterans like Steinhoff included, were also on a learning curve with tactics. The Me 262 at high speed was difficult to maneuver with high stress in turns and limited time in aiming, due to closing speeds, and even in attacks from the rear since the aircraft had no speed brakes. When armed with 24 rockets, the 262 attacks from the rear, like Der Sturmgruppen, were devastating. The cost was high. Much of the crème was gone. Luetzow was dead, and Steinhoff, the horribly burned survivor of a crash on 18 April, was recovering in an American military hospital.

It was late April 1945, much too little and much too late to make any difference in the air battle or, for that matter, the war. Germany lay in ruins. Russian and Allied forces were converging on Berlin. Hitler would soon be dead and Berlin overrun with Russian looting and rape. The Eighth Air Force continued relentlessly with 17 missions to Germany from April 3 through the 25th, daily from April 3-11 and from April 16-21. Most of these missions were with 1,000 plus bombers in multiple formations. All were against targets in Germany at a cost of 101 bombers and 88 fighters. The last bombing mission to a German target was on 25 April 1945. One can only guess as to whether or not the Me 262 might have made a significant difference in the air battle, but even then only as a forerunner of things to come – certainly not in the outcome of the war. What 25 April 1945 does symbolize is the end of the U.S.-British air campaign in Western Europe.

CHAPTER 20   PRISONERS OF WAR

The March Of Death

By January 1945, Germany was about to be overrun from the east and the west in the claws of a giant crustacean, with the Russians sweeping through Poland toward Berlin and the Allies on the banks of the Rhine. It was abundantly clear that these thrusts into the heart of the Reich would not be stopped until Berlin fell. Western Europe was also in the grip of one of the coldest winters on record. In the face of the Russian spearheads, anarchy would overtake the German people of Pomarania and East Prussia – now essentially refugees fleeing in a mass exodus toward Berlin and choking the roads with meager possessions in tow. It was into this chaotic morass that Adolph Hiller stepped when he made a decision to move POWs in Luftwaffe-run Stalag Lufts to the west. I regard this as something of an enigma, wondering what Hitler had in mind. It would seem plausible under the circumstances to simply let the Russians deal with the tasks of feeding, housing, and clothing thousands of Allied prisoners and arranging for their repatriation to their mother countries. The answer I subscribe to, however, suggests that the wily Hitler had, typically for Hitler, a brutal objective – his aim was to hold the POWs hostage by billeting them in German cities under relentless bombing attacks with the idea that the bombing might end in a step to protect Allied prisoners so confined. If the bombing did not end, then Hitler would have them executed.

What followed was an exercise in unmitigated brutality that has not been fully aired or appreciated. It is known as "the march of death," comparable to Bataan in terms of bestiality but in some cases even a broader span of distance and duration-bearing misery, in one case over 80 days. Bataan may have the edge in pure savagery characterized by brutal physical abuse and murder. The Bataan death march spanned 80 miles with 60,000 to 80,000 Americans and Filipinos. Numbers are uncertain, but up to 650 Americans perished – with no definitive records, 2,500 to as many as 10,000 Filipinos died.

There were 95,000 Americans among the minions of German prisoners. Of these, 38,000 were airmen – 28,000 from bomber crews and the remainder fighter pilots.

The exodus of misery began with orders to evacuate Stalag Luft III on 27 January as the Russians were closing in on Posen and Breslau. Hitler directed the Luftwaffe to move prisoners of Stalag Luft III to camps near Berlin, some 100 miles distant. Stalag III was near the town of Sagan in Lower Silesia – now in Poland. Its claim to fame is the 1963 film "The Great Escape," with the camp's three tunnels, "Tom," "Dick," and "Harry," through which 76 escaped with 73 recaptured and 50 of those executed courtesy of Heinrich Himmler of Hitler's SS brutes. The "kriegies," as they were called, were given 30 minutes to take whatever they could carry and assemble in the snow at the front gate. A contingent of 2,000 under the leadership of Col Darr Alkire were the first to leave the compound. The last to leave were led by General Arthur Vanaman. The trek of the first group began in blinding snow without food or water and ended on 1 February at Stremberg, where it was learned that they would by packed in unheated cattle cars called 40X8s (40 men, eight horses) – up to 60 men and sometimes more in each car and in unbearable conditions. Their destination was Stalag VIIA near the town of Moosburg in eastern Bavaria where a large camp awaited them. Stalag VIIA was designed to hold about 6000 kriegies; when liberated on 29 April 1945 it is estimated that there were more than 80,000 inmates. Hordes of prisoners from other evacuated Stalags descended on Moosburg where they would live in appalling conditions until liberated by American troops.

None of the POWs that moved west would suffer any worse than the men of Stalag Luft IV located in East Prussia. There were over 9,000 prisoners confined there – mostly American non-commissioned officers and other ranks plus some Britons and Canadians. When the evacuation began, 2,000 sick and wounded Stalag Luft IV POWs were moved by train in unheated 40X8s freight cars – packed as human herds in the epitome of unspeakable conditions.

On 6 February 1945 the order was given to move the remaining 6,000 by foot. Consider now the brutal weather and what lay ahead for unfed, ill clad and barely shod men who would suffer through starvation, sickness and brutality over a distance of some 600 miles in a span of 86 days. The kriegies reached Stalag XI-B near Fallingostel, Germany where they were folded into a large camp with other prisoners. Treatment followed those of previous patterns – even worse because of the lack of food. But by early May the sounds of American artillery were now being heard. The Stalag IV POWs were in this camp for about one week when they marched again for about three weeks, when on 2 May 1945 they were liberated by the British troops near the river Elba at Lauenburg, Germany. Of the 6,000 who began the 86 day trek of misery, 1,300 would die.

Zemke's Stalag

Another tale of a Stalag Luft has drawn my interest because of its contrasts and the outcome. Stalag I, located at Barth on the Baltic Sea, was considered an airmens' camp of aces by the Luftwaffe. Among the aces were Lt Col Hubert "Hub" Zemke with 20 victories, Lt Col Francis Gabreski, holder of 28 kills, and other notables: Lt Col Charles Ross who led a flight on the Doolittle Tokyo raid, and John Morgan, holder of the Medal of Honor. When Zemke arrived in December 1944, by seniority he became the senior officer in charge of some 9,000 inmates. A significant contrast to Stalag Luft IV was that Zemke's "kriegies" were spared the cruelties and horrors of a winter march – they were still behind barbed wire at Barth.

The son of German immigrant parents, Zemke was born in Missoula, Montana in 1914, and was bilingual, an asset that would serve him well in years to come as a German POW. Zemke entered the U.S. Army Air Corps Aviation Cadet Program in 1936 at Randolph Field in Texas, graduating in 1937 as a second lieutenant pilot. Following graduation he was assigned to the 36th Pursuit Squadron as a P-40 pilot. In 1940 he served briefly with the RAF as an observer studying both RAF and Luftwaffe tactics. In 1941 he was sent to the Soviet Union to instruct Russian pilots in the P-40 aircraft then being sent to the Soviet Union under the Lend-Lease program, yielding another language asset he would use later.

Hub Zemke went on to grow with the expanding USAAF and took command of the P-47 equipped 56th Fighter Group, Eighth Air Force Fighter Command – "The Wolf Pack." Zemke's insights into the performance characteristics of the P-47 allowed him to raise its strengths above its limitations – the bounce and run tactics described earlier. While under his leadership, the 56th became a leading fighter group. He made the transition later to P-51s serving with 479th Group. On 30 October 1944, Zemke encountered severe turbulence in a P-51 that resulted in the loss of a wing, forcing him to bail out over enemy territory. He was captured and incarcerated in Stalag Luft I located at Barth. Of 9,000 POWs in the complex, 7,588 Americans and 1,351 British and Canadian airmen. Zemke, more importantly had another human asset, he was a study in that rare quality called leadership.

As leader of the POWs, Zemke's command of the German language enabled a working relationship with the Luftwaffe officer commanding the complex. With the Soviet Army now approximately 25 miles distant, using his fluent German, Zemke made contact with the camp commander and convinced him that it was pointless for commander and his limited capability to oppose the overwhelming Russian force approaching from the east. He suggested that the German commander and guards leave armaments behind and evacuate with their side arms. He, Zemke, would be left in charge to deal with the Russians. When the Russians overran the town and the camp, their behavior descended into a chaotic pattern of pillage and rape. With no order of discipline or control, the communities bordering the camp morphed into uncontrollable bedlam. Zemke's problem was to keep his POWs from joining the chaos. He also had to deal with the Russians in a negotiating mode to arrange for moving his charges to U.S. controlled territory some 400 miles distant – bear in mind that Barth was now in Russian territory. In the ensuing negotiation with his Russian counterpart, Zemke was told that evacuation by air was not possible because of an agreement prohibiting U. S. aircraft from flying over Russian territory. Thus, the evacuation would have to be overland to the Black Sea. However, in Zemke's further attempts to cut a deal, the Russians agreed to an airlift if the U.S would surrender a Red Army commander named Andre Vlasov. The Red commander had been captured by the Germans and defected; he then formed a force of Russian prisoners who he would lead in an effort to bring down Stalin. It was a piece of cake; the Russians really wanted Vlasov. When he was turned over to the Russians, a pre- planned signal was given to start the airlift that would be dubbed "Operation Revival." This was accomplished by B-17 aircraft that were flown in an airlift operation numbering some 300 flights. Zemke arranged for the British POWs to go first since they had been in captivity the longest. The American POWs were evacuated the next day by a fleet of B-17s landing in one minute intervals. The POWs and the B-17s crews recovered at an airfield near Le Havre; the POWs then boarded a train for Camp Lucky Strike where they were fed, clothed, and received medical attention in preparation for going home.

Douglas Bader

There is a mystical bonding quality in soldiering seen repeatedly in the annals of military history – one that crosses the borders of contending enemies on the fields of battle. In my own experience, I never thought of German airmen as Nazi ogres but rather in terms of fearful respect. As noted earlier, Eighth Air Force radio operator Sgt J. J. Lynch said it best – we were all captured by the same madness of the war that swept our generation away. A powerful and most intriguing example of this phenomenon is that of Luftwaffe pilot and ace Franz Stigler, who spared a crippled B-17 over Germany and flew on its wing saluting the pilot rather than responding to his duty to destroy it.

In this chapter dealing with consummate brutality heaped upon Allied POWs as the war wound toward its conclusion, there is a counterpoint to all that discretionary violence in the story of RAF pilot Douglas Bader. Of all the names surfacing in the Battle of Britain and ensuing combat, perhaps no name is better known than that of Bader, who joined the RAF in 1928. Bader was commissioned as a fighter pilot in 1930. A year later, while performing acrobatics, he crashed, and as a result lost both legs.

Following the loss of his legs, Bader was given a medical retirement from the RAF. However, when the war started, he rejoined the RAF as an active fighter pilot when he convinced the medical examiners that activation of the rudder pedals in an aircraft required only a pushing motion which he could perform with artificial legs as easily as he could with real ones. Thus he returned to active status with the RAF as a fighter pilot; in Chapter 3 we saw his involvement in the Battle of Britain.

Bader's unusual story begins in August 1941 when he was shot down over Germany. When he bailed out of his burning aircraft, his right prosthetic leg became trapped in the aircraft, and he escaped only when the leg's retaining straps snapped after he pulled the ripcord on his parachute. Bader was captured when he landed. German forces treated Bader with great respect. General Adolf Galland, Luftwaffe ace and its leader, notified the British of his damaged leg and offered them safe passage to drop off a replacement. Hermann Goering approved the operation. The British responded on 19 August 1941 with the "Leg Operation" – an RAF bomber was allowed to drop a new prosthetic leg by parachute to St Omer, a Luftwaffe base in occupied France, as part of Circus 81 involving six Bristol Blenheims and a sizeable fighter escort.

Subsequently, in spite of his disability, Bader made several unsuccessful attempts to escape, and as a result was transferred to the Luftwaffe's maximum security POW camp at Colditz Castle – reserved for "incorrigibles" – where he remained until April 1945 when liberated by the U.S. Army

Bader was an RAF ace credited with 20 victories. He retired from the RAF in February 1946 and died of a heart attack on 5 September 1982 at the age of 72.

Author with artist Matt Holness, June 2013

Holness Collection

EPILOGUE

I will make war
No more forever

Chief Joseph, Nez Perce Tribe

As the Allied strategic bombing campaign entered 1945, both the RAF Bomber Command and the Eighth Air Force were pounding German cities at will. Perhaps the most infamous Allied air attacks of the war were those of the RAF and Eighth Air Force on Dresden early in February (See Chapter 4).

It is difficult to imagine the casualties suffered by the Eighth Air Force through the three years of its wartime operations in Europe. Over 47,000 (bombers and fighters) were dead or missing according to Roger Freeman. That is a fearsome number. The Eighth Air Force suffered more casualties than any other Army, Navy, or Marine unit of comparable size in WW II. RAF Bomber Command casualties over a 6 year period were even worse – 55,573.

Perhaps the critical question is: what did it all accomplish? By 8 May 1945 – Victory in Europe (VE) Day – the Eighth Bomber Command alone had dumped 692,918 tons of bombs on targets in Western Europe. That, combined with much more tonnage dumped by the RAF, left German cities lying in heaps of rubble.

Unquestionably, the impact of this application of air power was a factor in Germany's ultimate defeat. Yet it was the elimination of the Wehrmacht in the field by Allied ground forces that brought the war to its final conclusion. That could not have been accomplished without the overwhelming air support provided. Thus one was dependent on the other.

The great air war was over in Europe. Strategic bombing in concept had, never been fully demonstrated. Paradoxically, in spite of all the devastating night and day attacks in 1944 against Germany's war industries and her cities, production of aircraft and V2 weapons actually increased. In an article in the February 1996 issue of *The 8ᵗʰ AF News*, the editor quotes statements made by Hermann Goering shortly after the war and before he poisoned himself while awaiting judgment at Nuremberg. Goering recognized that the Luftwaffe was losing the air war as soon as Eighth Air Force escort fighters made their appearance. Yet he was convinced that German jet fighters could again turn the air war in Germany's favor. Jet aircraft production had gone underground, as did other war industries. Goering stated further that pilot training output was always ahead of the jet aircraft production. Based on assessments by Galland and others, Goering's conclusion on pilot training is hardly plausible. Goering said further, "Germany could not have been defeated with air power alone, using England as a base, without invasion because German industry was going underground."

Goering went on to acknowledge that the land invasion of Western Europe drained workers from factory production as well as human resources for the Luftwaffe. Further, "Allied precision bombing had a greater effect than area bombing, because destroyed cities could be evacuated, but destroyed industry was hard to replace. Allied selection of targets was good, particularly in regard to oil. As soon as we started to repair an oil installation, you always bombed it again before we could produce one ton. The Allies owe the success of the invasion to the air forces. Without the U.S. Air Force the war would still be going on elsewhere, but certainly not on German soil."

Goering's track record does not necessarily elevate him to the upper levels of wisdom for commenting on the results of the air war, but he was certainly a key figure on the losing side. The debates can be endless. Nor is any of it relevant to this work, but it took me fifty years to get it all in perspective. I leave the whole business in the words of George S. Patton: "The truth about a war was never known until one hundred years after it was over, until everyone who had fought in it was dead."

Looking back through an aviation career spanning over 40 years, I have come to realize that my brief encounter with the Eighth Air Force had a profound effect that would follow me into my ensuing flying career and careers thereafter. Some of it was very negative, as the worst fears of combat were somehow transferred to the active USAF flying career that ensued after my tour with the Eighth. I entered my post-England world of aviation with my acquired skills and knowing a lot about combat operations, but I had yet to gain the wisdom and experience that would one day make me an old pilot. It did not take me long to realize that my piloting skills were very limited.

As a transport pilot after the war, I can remember countless occasions in C-54s in take-off position awaiting Air Traffic Control clearance for departure on North Atlantic crossings. With 42 dependent souls behind me, I wondered why my palms were wet. I sensed anxieties as I contemplated one or more of a host of hazards that I had to deal with – penetrating the squall line that lay across my flight path, destination weather deterioration, severe turbulence, icing, engine failures, decision points en route, unreliable communications. In a sense some of these things became substitutes for the German flak and fighters I faced during my combat missions. Such sensations would rapidly evaporate as I rolled the aircraft on the active runway and advanced the throttles for the departure. Once airborne, I was a different person, focused and in command. Yet I felt as if I were on some kind of emotional roller coaster at such moments.

In Summary, Some Observations

The divergent paths of the RAF Bomber Command and the Eighth Air Force Bomber Command continued through VE Day. Harris's focus on German cities was only partially effective. Major goals were never reached, especially that of terrorizing civil populations in those cities.

Harris was redirected to strategic objectives after D-Day, but city bombing continued. Likewise, Eighth Air Force objectives were only partially successful. While precision strikes disruptive, German industrial production continued as factories went underground. It was the disruption of oil production and transportation that brought on Germany's final collapse, to say nothing of the Russians sweep into Germany.

Doolittle's objective was to take out the Luftwaffe before D-Day and his decision to release escort fighters from Eighth Bomber Command's formations hastened the end. P-51 and P-47 "fighter sweeps" were intercepting Luftwaffe fighters as they assembled and shot up anything that moved on the way out. Bomber tracks into target areas were elongated to flush out German fighters to their destruction.

Big Week, launched by the Eighth Air Force in February 1944, ushered in a pattern of deadly aerial combat that led to the decline and eventual defeat of the Luftwaffe. This was evident on D-Day, as the Luftwaffe never showed up. Had they been able to mount strong fighter-bomber attacks on the landing beaches, the outcome might have been different.

The Eighth Bomber Command was on its knees at the end of 1943 due to unacceptable attrition, this in turn due to the lack of escort fighters for deep penetration. The development of the North American P-51 solved this problem and was a key factor in the defeat of the Luftwaffe.

Oil production was recognized as a key target from the outset – e.g., Ploesti. Focusing renewed emphasis on German oil and synthetic fuel output in May 1944 accelerated Germany's ultimate demise.

The shift in targeting after D-Day to transportation facilities resulted in extensive damage to Germany's war effort, especially in industrial output and troop deployments. Heavy bombers were focusing on transportation hubs, but Ninth Air Force B-26s and especially the heavily armed P-47s wreaked havoc on German movement after D-Day and provided close support for infantry operations.

Radar navigation and target location by the RAF in night bombing operations became Harris's ace in the hole in finding and destroying German cities. Radar use by Eighth Bomber Command was introduced in the spring of 1944 and became the norm as operations continued, in essence relegating the Eighth to "carpet bombing."

In one speculative assessment, it would seem that the USAAF's commitment to pinpoint bombing was eventually abandoned. Area bombing, brought on initially with the expanded use of radar, surfaced in Western Europe but continued on against Tokyo with B-29s and the introduction of the atomic bomb.

Hitler's meddlesome decision-making regarding Luftwaffe strategy was among the Allies' greatest assets. By diverting attacks on RAF airfields and industries in the Battle of Britain to bombing London and other British cities, the invasion of England became the invasion that never was. Hitler's failure to turn the Panzers loose on D-Day negated any possibility of stopping the Allied invasion of Normandy. Hitler's proposed misuse of the Me 262, negated any possibility of stopping attacks by the Eighth Bomber Command.

Herman Goering's inability to understand contemporary fighter tactics contributed to the Luftwaffe's defeat in the Battle of Britain. His failure to support Adolf Galland in employing the Me 262 as a fighter removed any hope of stopping or curtailing daylight bombing.

The cost of all this in terms of human life is unimaginable. WW II casualties below do not include USAAF 15th Air Force, 9th Air Force, or Troop Carrier Command losses. The focus is on the RAF, Luftwaffe, and the Eighth Air Force in line with the author's thesis.

WW II Casualties: Great Britain, Germany, and United States Air Forces		
Group	Number Killed	Timeframe
Battle of Britain		
RAF Pilots	537	July-December 1940
Civilians	23,000	July-December 1940
Blitz, Civilians, London alone	50,000	September 1940-May 1941
RAF Bomber Command	55,573	1939-September 1945
USAAF Eight Air Force	47,000	1942-1945
Luftwaffe	453,000	1939-1945
German Civilian	600,000	1941-1945
Civilians in Other Countries	Undetermined	1939-1945

Something like a veil of silence seems to fall like a pall over the issue of morality. One of the great dilemmas of mass bombing in WW II lies in the absence of accountability. It is not as though there were no voices raised in protest; they were, in fact, largely ignored, both in the UK and in the U.S. The fact is that everybody knew that bombing killed innocents, but public opinion during the war supported the simple truth that Hitler, with all the terror and destruction wrought by his armies, must be defeated at any cost. In America, public awareness of mass killing was muted by distance to some extent —Americans were not subjected to the realities of the carnage seen in Europe.

Emanating from the theorists, Douhet in particular, was the concept that total war justified attacks on cities. City people, along with armies in the field, are ingrained into the conflict. Consider Russia and the "scorched earth" policy. Bombing Germany was accepted accordingly. Not only the public, but our military and political leaders were well aware of the consequences of falling bombs in cities, even where precision strikes were intended to minimize casualties. But fire-bombing cities, with the idea of destroying them to take out industry and labor forces, brought the reality of total war into the equation. Civilian casualties were the accepted trade off. Focusing on cities was considered the ultimate path to the war's end.

The raids went on, and the political leaders remained hidden behind the men who implemented their strategy. Worse, it seems like the moral imperative has yet to be learned. Thoughts here turn to Bagdad when it went under "shock and awe" air attacks in 2003 with modern weapons — the trade off again at work.

We learn from history what we do not learn from history.

Georg Friederich Wilhelm Hegel

Appendix 1:   Research Sources

Chapter 1

The Great Air War, The Men, The Planners, The Saga of Military Aviation 1914-1918, Norman, Aaron; The Macmillan Company 1968

Chapter 2

Lancaster, The Biography, Squadron Leader Iveson, Tony; Carlton Publishing Group 2009

With Wings Like Eagles, A History of the Battle of Britain Korda, Michael; Success Research Corporation 2009

Chapter 3

With Wings Like Eagles, A History of the Battle of Britain, Korda, Michael; Success Research Corporation 2009

Chapter 4

Lancaster, The Biography, Squadron Leader Iveson, Tony; Carlton Publishing Group 2009

The Invention that Changed the World, Buderi, Robert, Simon and Schuster 1996

The Mighty Eighth 1986, *The Mighty Eighth War Diary,* 1981, *The Mighty Eighth War Manual,* 1987, Freeman, Roger; Jane's Information Group, Inc.

Masters of the Air, American Bomber Boys Who Fought the Air War Against Nazi Germany, Miller, Donald L.; Simon and Schuster 2006

Fire and Fury, the Allied Bombing of Germany 1942-1945, Hansen, Randall; NAL Caliber/Penguin Group 2009

Clash of Wings, Boyne, Walter; Simon and Schuster 1994

Chapter 5

An Assessment of the Principles of War on the Anglo-American Combined Bomber Offensive in Europe During World War II, 1942-1945, Asher, Susan P. Lt Col USAF (Retired)

Hitler's Luftwaffe, Tony Wood and Bill Gunston; Salamander Books Ltd. 1997

Military Heritage of America, R. Ernest Dupuy and Trevor N. Dupuy; McGraw- Hill 1956

Chapter 6

Masters of the Air, American Bomber Boys Who Fought the Air War Against Nazi Germany, Miller, Donald L.; Simon and Schuster 2006

The Mighty Eighth 1986, *The Mighty Eighth War Diary*, 1981, *The Mighty Eighth War Manual*, 1987, Freeman, Roger; Jane's Information Group, Inc.

Chapter 7

Impact Magazine, Volume 5, 1945 – USAAF Gen Curtis LeMay

The Bombing of Germany, Rumpf, Hans; White Lion Publishers 1963
Chapter 10

Clash of Wings, Boyne, Walter; Simon and Schuster 1994

Masters of the Air, American Bomber Boys Who Fought the Air War Against Nazi Germany, Miller, Donald L.; Simon and Schuster 2006

The Mighty Eighth 1986, *The Mighty Eighth War Diary*, 1981, *The Mighty Eighth War Manual*, 1987, Freeman, Roger;   Jane's Information Group, Inc.

Chapter 11

Masters of the Air, American Bomber Boys Who Fought the Air War Against Nazi Germany, Miller, Donald L.; Simon and Schuster 2006

Chapter 12

The Mighty Eighth 1986, *The Mighty Eighth War Diary*, 1981, *The Mighty Eighth War Manual*, 1987, Freeman, Roger; Jane's Information Group, Inc.

Masters of the Air, American Bomber Boys Who Fought the Air War Against Nazi Germany, Miller, Donald L.; Simon and Schuster 2006

Chapter 13

Fire and Fury, The Allied Bombing of Germany 1942-1945, Hansen, Randall NAL Caliber/Penguin Group 2009

The Mighty Eighth 1986, *The Mighty Eighth War Diary*, 1981, *The Mighty Eighth War Manual*, 1987, Freeman, Roger; Jane's Information Group, Inc.

Chapter 14

V Missiles of the Third Reich – The V-1 and V-2, Hoelsken, Dieter; Monogram Aviation Publications 1994

Chapter 17

The Mighty Eighth 1986, *The Mighty Eighth War Diary*, 1981, *The Mighty Eighth War Manual*, 1987, Freeman, Roger; Jane's Information Group, Inc.

The Final Hours, A German Jet Pilot Plots Against Goering, Steinhoff, Johannes; The Nautical and Aviation Publishing Company of America 1974

Chapter 18

The Mighty Eighth 1986, *The Mighty Eighth War Diary*, 1981, *The Mighty Eighth War Manual*, 1987, Freeman, Roger; Jane's

Information Group, Inc.

Wikipedia

The History of the 487th Bomb Group (H), Ivo De Jung, Turner Publishing Company, Tennessee – Paducha, Kentucky

Masters of the Air, American Bomber Boys Who Fought the Air War Against Nazi Germany, Miller, Donald L.; Simon and Schuster 2006

Chapter 19

The Final Hours, A German Jet Pilot Plots Against Goering, Steinhoff, Johannes; The Nautical and Aviation Publishing Company of America 1974

Chapter 20

Masters of the Air, American Bomber Boys Who Fought the Air War Against Nazi Germany, Miller, Donald L.; Simon and Schuster 2006

Appendix 2: Comparative Data Between the B-24 and B-17

B-24 vs B-17 Characteristics and Performance		
Characteristic	B-24H	B-17G
Engines	4 P&W 1830, 1200 hp	4 Wright 1820, 1200 hp
Wing Span	110 ft	103 ft 9 in
Wing Area (sq ft)	1,048	1,420
Empty Weight	36,500 lbs	36,135 lbs
Maximum Gross Weight	67,800 lbs	65,500 lbs
Fuel Capacity (U.S. gallons)	2,794	2,780
Maximum Speed	290 mph at 25,000 ft	287 mph at 25,000 ft
Tactical Operating Speed	205 mph at 25,000 ft	180-215 mph at 25,000 ft
Service Ceiling	28,000 ft	37,500
Tactical Altitude	18,000-22,000 ft	21,000-27,000 ft
Normal Range	2,100 miles	2,000 miles
Tactical Radius	700 miles	650-800 miles
Maximum Bomb Load	12,800 lbs	13,600 lbs
Normal Tactical Bomb Load	5,000 lbs	4,000 lbs
Armament	10 x .50 in mg	12 x .50 in mg
Crew	10	10
Sources: *The Mighty Eighth*, Roger Freeman, *Jane's Fighting Aircraft of WW II*, Pilot Training Manuals – B-17 and B-24		
Note: The author flew both aircraft in combat		

All range and altitude performance numbers given are loaded with variables and are suspect. Altitude, operating weight, "tactical"

245

speeds, and fuel consumption govern comparative performance in terms of range. One way to compare these parameters would be to plot maximum range based on the maximum gross weights and fuel loads of the two aircraft at their respective "tactical" operating altitudes – 22,000 feet for the B-24 and 27,000 feet for the B-17. Both are flying at "tactical" operating speeds of 160 mph and 150 mph IAS respectively. The true air speed (IAS corrected for air density and temperature) of the B-17 is higher than that of the B-24 at tactical altitudes (27,000 feet vs 22,000 feet). Another variable is fuel consumption. The B-24 required higher engine power settings at 22,000 feet than the B-17 at 27,000 feet, with higher fuel consumption as a result. Fuel capacities are essentially the same. Thus, with lower fuel consumption and a higher true air speed, the B-17 goes farther.

A significant factor in the performance of the two aircraft at high altitude in combat was the wing area of each – 1,048 sq. ft. for the B-24 and 1,420 sq. ft. for the B-17. The B-24 had a wider span and the touted Davis Airfoil designed for high lift performance, which proved disappointing. The B-17 had more lift area which gave it an altitude edge over the B-24 and better performance in terms of fuel consumption and radius of action. The B-17 was far easier to handle in formation at tactical altitudes given in the table.

Appendix 3: Missions

Missions Flown in 1944 by Lt Bernard Nolan with the 487th Bomb Group, Eighth Air Force.

1944 Missions, Lt Bernard Nolan			
B-24H 45-52748 Missions			
Mission No.	**Date**	**Target Location**	**Target Type**
1	9 May	Lyon, France	Airfield
2	24 May	Paris, France	Orly Airfield
3	28 May	Lutzkendorf, Germany	Oil Refinery
4	31 May	Jemelle, Belgium	Marshaling Yards
5	6 June	Thury-Hancourt, France	Railroad Bridge
6	7 June	Montjeau, France	Bridge
7	8 June	Cinq Mars, Fr	Bridge
8	11 June	Argentan, France	Airfield
9	12 June	Beauvais-Nevellers, France	Airfield
10	14 June	Lille-Venderville, France	Airfield
11	15 June	Etampes-Mondesir, France	Airfield

12	17 June	Alencon, France	Airfield
13	20 June[1]	Misburg, Germany	Oil Refinery
14[3]	20 June[1]	Pas de Calais, France	V-1 Weapons Site
15	22 June	Pas de Calais, France	V-1 Weapons Site
16	23 June	Colommiers, France	Airfield
17[3]	24 June	Chateaudun, France	Airfield
18[3]	30 June	Conches, France	Airfield
19	8 July[2]	Laloge-au-Pain, France	Weapon Site
20	14 July	Peronne, France	Airfield
21	17 July	Gien, France	Bridge
22	18 July	Frenouville, France	Troop Concentration

B-17G 46307 Missions

23	1 August	Tours, France	Airfield
24	5 August	Magdeburg, Germany	Airplane Factory
25	6 August	Berlin, Germany	Industrial Plant
26	7 August	Jussy, France	Railroad bridge
27	9 August	Nurnburg, Germany	Ball Bearing Plant
28	16 August	Rositz, Germany	Oil Refinery
29	24 August	Freital, Germany	Oil Refinery

30	25 August	Rechlin/Peenamunde, Germany	Experimental Site
31	26 August	Brest, France	Coastal Defenses
32	1 September	Russelsheim, Germany	?
33	9 September	Dusseldorf, Germany	Coastal Defenses

[1] Flew two missions on June 20

[2] Note Shot down crossing the coast at Ostend, Belgium, Recovered in England RAF Bradwell Bay

[3] Missions on 14, 17 and 18 July flown in replacement B-24H

Bernard T. Nolan's entire life has been spent in aerospace related activities including 22 years in the USAF as an active pilot. He flew 33 missions in B-24s and B-17s with the 8th Bomber Command in Europe in 1944. Following his combat experiences, he was retrained as a transport pilot and flew North Atlantic and other routes for ten years. He had various program assignments in NASA, and after retirement worked as an independent consultant to NASA and as a senior engineer for the Science Applications International Corporation. He is also the author of *Isaiah's Eagles Rising: A Generation of Airmen*.

Matt Holness grew up in the South East of England in what they called during the Battle of Britain "Hells Corner," so aviation was always going to be in the blood from the start. Living next to RAF West Malling, deep in the Kent countryside during all his life, the passion for aviation took hold. Straight from school he completed his aircraft apprenticeship on air frames which lead into avionics and aircraft interiors, working for Hunting Aviation, Martin Baker Aircraft Ejection Seats, BAE SYSTEMS and Virgin Atlantic Airways. His passion for aviation art started at the same time and he now sells artwork all around the world, including the World Aviation Paintings of the Year Expo, held at the Mall Galleries in London. The front cover is based on an actual event Bernard Nolan experienced on 25 July 1944.

Miniver Press is a publisher of lively and informative non-fiction books based in McLean, Virginia. For more information, see http://www.miniverpress.com

21431868R00142

Made in the USA
Charleston, SC
16 August 2013